THE HARRAD LETTERS

Also by Robert H. Rimmer and available in the NEL series.

THE ZOLOTOV AFFAIR
PROPOSITION 31
THE REBELLION OF YALE MARRATT
THE HARRAD EXPERIMENT

The Harrad Letters

to

Robert H. Rimmer

NEW ENGLISH LIBRARY
TIMES MIRROR

First published in the United States of America by New American Library
© 1969 Robert H. Rimmer

*

FIRST NEL PAPERBACK EDITION FEBRUARY 1971

*

NEL Books are published by
New English Library Limited from Barnard's Inn, Holborn, London E.C.1.
Made and printed in Great Britain by Hunt Barnard Printing Ltd., Aylesbury, Bucks.

45000664 6

Contents

Apology from a Man
in Search of a Fulcrum

1

If you are under thirty (or even over thirty and can shake the lethargy of your hoary longevity), this is your book. You may be one of the thousands of enthusiastic readers of *The Harrad Experiment*, *The Rebellion of Yale Marratt*, or *Proposition 31* who have personally written me, telephoned me from every state in the country, or tracked me down to my office, where I run a business that has absolutely nothing to do with writing or publishing. Or you may be one of the several million who have purchased *The Harrad Experiment* or *Yale Marratt*, and being a little more conservative have cheered silently (or with reservations) and have told your friends this is a book *they* should read. Whoever you are, you created a publishing phenomenon that for better or worse may have changed not only your life a little, but mine, too! An unknown, unreviewed book, published by a small West Coast company in hardcover after it had been rejected by such affluents in the publishing field as Bernard Geis and Barney Rossett, within eighteen months after paperback publications has sold more than two million copies in the United States and England, has been translated into Japanese, German, and Italian, and may continue to sell for years to come—at least until a Harrad College becomes a reality, or man has discovered some other way of humanizing the male-female relationship.

Most of this book consists of letters from you to me. I doubt that many authors of novels, best-selling or otherwise, receive this kind of intimate, personal mail from readers. I think the reason, as much as the book itself, is the biographical note that appears at the end of *The Harrad Experiment*: "Bob Rimmer is a man who thinks he can move the world and is busily trying to find a place to put the fulcrum." I'm chuckling as I write this because the truth is that I have no pretensions to grandeur or fame. In fact, in the past two years as I slowly discovered that I might well become engulfed by people seeking me out, I have occasionally thought, like J. D. Salinger or Howard Hughes, I would disappear from public view. Not really. . . . I'm too people oriented. I love you and myself because we are human beings who occasionally surpass ourselves and act like benevolent gods.

So, while I have answered everyone who has written me, the answers were often limited. In truth, some of your questions would require a book to answer. This book then serves a triple purpose. It's my opportunity to be defenseless before you, assure you that in your joyous idealism you are not alone, and thank you. I believe in *you*! Whether or not there is a God in the universe, I am not concerned. *You*, amazing male, amazing female, with potentials within yourselves that you have only begun to explore, are a sufficient mystery, joy, and ecstasy to fill a lifetime. I'm glad to be alive in your world!

Of course, it's not the best of all possible worlds. But with a proper historical perspective on changing human values it's a lot better world than it ever has been at any time in human history. And thank God it isn't Utopia. A few years ago, because a great many people considered me a Utopian novelist, I started reading every possible Utopian conception of man. Believe me, if I understand you, you wouldn't want to live in Utopia. Everything would be perfect. Analyze that word "perfect." It's beyond improvement. Perfect may well equal dull!

You and I are living at a fascinating time . . . not the best of times and not the worst. Fascinating because we are at the confluence of history. A predetermination perhaps that the common man, painfully conquering his environment, would eventually triumph over nature and realize himself in an entirely new dimension. A "now" time, where his very survival depends on a deep understanding and brotherhood with his fellowman. We have arrived. We are the vertical invasion of the masses that Ortega y Gasset prophesied. With vast technologies that we have created but have not yet learned to put to human uses, we have emerged from the dark, safe womb of the past into the blazing sunlight of our possibilities.

Is it any wonder we are stumbling? We are freer men and women than have ever existed in this world. In the desperate fight, century by century, to shake off the tyrannies of religions and governments (really man trying to control man and make a society) we have arrived at a juncture in history where most of the values of the past are inadequate to the present. But it's nothing to fear. Rather it's the time to experiment and discard, until slowly

8

out of the experimentation we create the world of the future. If you stop to think, isn't it even more exciting to lay the groundwork for the future you may never live to see than actually live in it? Remember, if you live another fifty years you'll have to face the bad decisions you made.

2

I can't help it. I keep writing as if you are under thirty. Maybe, like me, you are well past thirty. But it's quite unlikely that like me you are over fifty. If you are, welcome to a very small club! Most of my contemporaries are men who don't read books ... especially books about sex and love. In fact, we seem to be living in a culture where the idea of sexual love past fifty is somewhat embarrassing. The sad truth is that if I depended on my own age group for friends I would be bereft. Largely, we can't talk to each other. When I am on the side of the college rioters (better complaint than apathy) or have a suspicion that if I were born Stokely Carmichael or Mao Tse-tung I might well emulate their behavior, I find that I'm often in danger of bursting the tired blood vessels of my fellow senior citizens. My God ... is it a condition of man that when he passes a certain age he can no longer empathize?

So, if you are under thirty the warning should be apparent to you. In 1972 50 percent of the population of the United States will be under twenty-five. For the next twenty-five years, *you* will dominate the world, and then by the turn of the century, with the driving necessity for population control, you and most of the United States will be the older generation.

"What can I do now?" If there is one question that I have been asked a thousand times in the past two years, that's the question.

I may disappoint you. I don't really believe that you and I can change the world. But, more important, we can change ourselves, and the aggregation of the change will in a generation or less completely change the world as we know it. Perhaps the best way I can answer the questions raised by the books I have written is to do what most people often fail to do with another human being. Be defenseless before you ... stop the role playing. It's quite amazing the responses you can evoke from another person if you *dare* to be the person you really are.

A few months ago I was invited to the Esalen Institute at Big Sun, California, to conduct a workshop titled *New*

Patterns in Love and Friendship. While I was familiar with the Esalen techniques, I had never participated in an unstructured encounter group. Twenty-two people, strangers to me, had paid $165 for a week to meet the author of *The Harrad Experiment* and *The Rebellion of Yale Marratt*. Because I have never considered myself a professional author, and because unlike the many psychologists, sociologists, and famous authors who conduct couples' groups and sensitivity-training workshops my only credentials were a Master's Degree in Business Administration, I felt quite inferior to what I assumed was expected from me. Barricaded behind a suitcase full of notes (my Maginot Line) with my group lying casually around the broadloomed floor of the Maslow Room, I opened the first session with a half-hour discussion of modern fiction interspersed with apologies that perhaps I was better trained to be running a seminar for businessmen and economists. When I finally relaxed and asked for questions, the first response took my breath away. A pretty blond junior from the University of Wisconsin looked at me with disappointment etched on her face. "I didn't come here to be lectured at. I read *The Harrad Experiment.* I love you. I want to know the real Bob Rimmer!" She was immediately cheered by the rest of the group. The barriers of communication were broken. We spent a joyous week in almost continuous sessions. Some of the meetings were with the entire group sandwiched together nude in the huge hot sulphur springs tubs. Slowly we discovered a swift and laughing way for human beings to relate to each other ... without drugs or alcohol.

So, who is the real Bob Rimmer? Who is the real you? It's the Socratic problem of "Know thyself," which most of us only vaguely attempt, and more often than not shy away from. Because *I* believe that individually we can't change the world is no reason to despair. We *can* manipulate our environment for self-actualization. My own background (so typically middle class) and my responses to it may give you some clues. In any event, I hope they may answer some of the questions readers of *Harrad*, *Yale Marratt*, and *Proposition 31* have asked me, and possibly reveal how it was possible for a man of forty-eight not only to write a book which the under-thirty generation could identify with, but point the way for *you* to live more fully in this new age of man.

All of us are products of our environment. But our reactions to the controlling aspects of it evolve out of ourselves. My father, who is eighty, went to work when he

10

was thirteen. At twenty-five, a graduate of the International Correspondence Schools, he married my mother, who was eighteen, a French Canadian. She had just emerged from a convent, with a poor command of English. With broken family backgrounds, a combination of questioning Protestant and Catholic, they fortunately didn't discover the "need" for structured religion until I was nine years old. A dedicated Christian Scientist adopted me for Sunday School. Christian Science Sunday School has one overwhelming value. You are expected to ask questions and you get reasonably straight answers. It was fortunately too late for indoctrination. Besides, my father, who rarely had time for reading, was vastly impressed with the importance of reading for his children. I had thoroughly digested Benjamin Franklin's *Autobiography* before I was ten. Coupled with Tom Swift, Horatio Alger, and Thomas Edison, the die was cast. Has anyone ever analyzed how much rebellion against the establishment is between the lines in these heroes of the 1920's? Inadvertently, I had acquired two positive value drives from my family. I had to find my own religion and I was conditioned that there were answers to everything. All I had to do was read all the books that had been written!

3

When I was finally accepted conditionally to Bates College, I had read more than the average senior ... in some areas. You will note the word "conditionally." I was deplorable at math. I wasn't even interested. There were no answers for me in algebra and geometry. In those days Bates was struggling. It was the Depression. If you could pay the tuition, you could go to college. Today, Bates and most colleges and universities would not accept a person like me. I cheer the campus rebels. Education is not a jigsaw puzzle composed of so many credits in the sciences, languages, mathematics, etc. In demanding more control of the educational processes today's students have recognized that the purpose of undergraduate education is integrating the whole man into a value structure that helps him realize himself as a human being.

Amusingly, perhaps because I was bugged by my own inability to grasp math, when my oldest boy was five years old, some twenty years later, I picked up an algebra and geometry text and discovered the concepts quite simple. Education is the teachers, too! I taught Bob Junior the rudiments of algebra when he was in the first grade.

"Education is at best ecstatic." Bob went on to the University of Pennsylvania and majored in math for two years until, *on his own*, like Bertrand Russell, he became convinced that too much math was a dead end. He switched to psychology, took four semesters of Russian, and ended up in medical school.

Is Bates College a prototype of Harrad College? Not then! Not now! But Bates *is* coed. In the years 1935 to 1939, when there were many more segregated male and female colleges than now, Bates didn't have the problem of girls visiting in the boys' dorms or vice versa. If you had a girl friend, you met her on the first floor of the dormitory, in a room provided for sit-up necking chaperoned by a house mother in her late fifties. Curfew was at ten o'clock. Since a vast majority of students "went steady" there was no place for sexual release except standing up in the shadows of the chapel. A common complaint of most male students in those days, though they were reluctant to admit it, was aching balls—a particularly grim affliction that most females are not familiar with and which can be relieved either by a female who is willing to help (some were, manually) or solitary masturbation.

Is campus life so different today? My guess is not essentially. In my college days we hadn't read Albert Kinsey, Ira Reiss, Albert Ellis, or Vance Packard. We had no one to lean on. We didn't even have much to read that was honestly sexual. Books like Faulkner's *Sanctuary*, Caldwell's *God's Little Acre*, and even Joyce's *Ulysses* circulated surreptitiously. We had no authority to justify our actions, but nevertheless most of the men I knew (myself included) before we had graduated had managed (usually in a car or in the woods or a shabby tourist cabin—they weren't called motels in those days) sexual intercourse with a female. Followed, depending on the time of month, by considerable worry over whether the rubbers had failed and we would have to get married. When the "curse" finally arrived (horrible word, that has fortunately disappeared), the male breathed a sigh of relief and was ready to gamble with fate again. Usually, quite traumatized by the fear of pregnancy out of wedlock, the female wasn't very cooperative! Did you ever read Thomas Hardy's *Jude the Obscure*? The 1930's weren't psychologically much different from the turn of the century.

Today, motels are fairly accessible, the pill is not too hard to come by, even parietal rules make it possible for reasonably comfortable copulation, and there are ten thousand books to assuage the conscience of the unmarried male and female, but my generation has pretty thoroughly transmitted the Christian-Judaistic guilt tradition. Despite the vast news coverage given the occasional students who move off campus and live together (unmarried or communally), my guess is that most males and females in their four year college experience have very limited sexual contacts. Those who do have made a mental commitment "to being in love" that usually neither party understands.

While the sexual revolution has made it possible to discuss sex freely and not get hung up on the virginity complexes of the past, my feeling is that the new female, freed of her dependency on the male both economically and from fear of pregnancy, still is pursuing the dream of monogamous marriage, and not until it is too late does she discover that neither she nor the male can cope with the new kind of "leaderless" marriage. The young female today won't tolerate the patriarchal family that gave a wobbly stability to her parents' marriage, and even if she would, the young male refuses to accept the dominant role.

Instead of a socially approved, structured form of premarital experimentation that would give the male and female an opportunity to adjust to their very new marital roles, all society offers is legal, monogamous marriage. Wouldn't it be more sane for a male and female to live together without legal entanglement and recognize marriage as the commitment a male and female make to society when they decide to have children?

4

Since *why* I wrote Harrad is related to my own process of self-discovery, let me continue for a moment the mental biography of a man, not too unlike the average man of today in a liberal arts college. I went to college with no real goals. I liked to read and I liked girls. Mostly I understood books better than girls. I thought I might like to write someday, but it was someday . . . not imminent. The largest political issue that students could relate to was "that man in the White House," Franklin Roosevelt, and the impossibility (discussed endlessly pro and con by debating teams) of the United States maintaining a thirty billion dollar debt, or the general wickedness of government going into business in such projects as the

Tennessee Valley Authority or harnessing the tide at Passamaquoddy, Maine, for electricity (an anathema to the Republican families of most Bates College students who lived in Maine). Hitler was a madman a million miles away. We watched his antics Saturday night on newsreels at the local movie house while we held hands and waited for the nice little sex comedies with Clark Gable, Jean Harlow, Franchot Tone, and Lana Turner. Betty Grable was the sex symbol. Most of my college generation never saw a live female naked . . . or even photographs of one with pubic hair.

I wrote short stories imitating Hemingway and Faulkner, which were published in the campus literary journal, and sold advertising for the college newspaper. I was finally offered the job of business manager of the paper. The first split between the real Bob Rimmer and reality had occurred. I would have preferred to be editor of the paper. I even had the necessary qualifications. But having a father who owned a small business, and with no real conviction of what I wanted to do in the world, I had acceded to parental direction, applied, and in my senior year had been accepted to Harvard Business School. The only overwhelming interest I had was being in love! In my last year at Bates, having completed my requirements for a major in English in my junior year, I switched to psychology and philosophy. In my senior year I was taking a mad mixture of economics, accounting, and advanced courses in psychology and philosophy. My closest friend, an assistant professor of psychology, felt that his prize student should be a teacher or even go to divinity school. But Harvard Business? Good Lord, No!

Please understand there is a point to this autobiography. Basically, it is not unusual; in fact, I believe it is quite typically average. Your father, if he is not an authoritarian figure and would dare to come down to earth, could duplicate or better it. It's the story of the average American trying to adjust his ideals and daydreams to the reality of making a living.

Not really a compromise. A truce with necessity. The compromise comes later. It's the compromise with living that most of my generation have made, and it's the compromise that you will make unless I can convince you you don't have to make it! *You* can live with your feet in two worlds. In fact, I predict that if you don't learn how to do this you will never change yourself or the world, and you will end up like most people I know in suburbia . . .

14

bored . . . living out their years in a futile chase of transient pleasures, wondering what life is all about.

I think I have avoided the compromise. Perhaps you won't agree. At the age of thirty-nine I decided to stop telling myself someday I would write. In March of 1957 I would be forty. I had spent sixteen years after graduation from Harvard continuing to read omnivorously not only in business areas but in practically every area of human knowledge. Like Thomas Wolfe wanting to read the entire Harvard library, I was possessed by a demon *to know*. To know what? I wasn't certain. Everything. If I were Faust, I too would have made a deal with Mephistopheles.

But in sixteen years, with the exception of a year or so in India and China at Uncle Sam's expense (we were fighting the Japanese then), I had written nothing but sales letters and advertising copy selling printing. Essentially, despite the necessity of making a living in the business world, I had soon come to the conclusion that I wasn't going to let the means become the ends and suppress my heritage (yours, too) as an intensely curious, wondering person. If I could avoid living it in one little bag, life would be endlessly fascinating. The world of business, making money, held moments of interest, but they were mostly transient . . . not vital, not ends in themselves. I could only laugh at the Harvard Business School dictum that the successful executive must plan to devote his life . . . ten waking hours a day . . . to his career. For what purpose? An article in *Dun's Review* (October, 1968), titled "Divorce Executive Style," presented one picture of the result:

Michael Smith, which is not his name, is the very model of a successful executive. Business acquaintances envy the ability and drive that made him executive vice president at the age of 37. His fellow executives talk about his devotion to the job . . . during his twelve years with the company his career has taken most of his time and energy. Mike spends grueling hours at the office, a great deal of his time travelling, and on weekends he pores over a stuffed briefcase. In the suburb where he, his wife and three children have lived for the past nine years, friends envy him his happy marriage. To them, hardworking Mike and his wife are the perfect couple living the perfect, all-American life. . . . Behind the happy facade Mike and his wife simply no longer care for

15

each other. In fact, they would like to separate. But they have played the game for some years now, and in all probability will go on playing it for many years longer. Not only do Mike and his wife "stick it out for the children's sake," there is also Mike's career to consider. ... The main cause of failure in such a marriage is, of course, the lack of communication between husband and wife. In this respect the executive is no different from any other. To some extent this breakdown in communication is caused by circumstance: he must devote a major part of his time to his job, and she must take care of the house and children. But the marriage is more often exacerbated by the personal factor which might be termed the executive ego. Notes Dr. Eugene Jennings, professor of administrative science at Michigan State University: "The all-American male ego says, 'If I tell my wife my fears, frustrations and anxieties, she will think I'm weak.'"

Note the words "*must devote* a major part of his time" in this quotation. If they are true, something is really wrong with the structure of business and commerce. Ends are confused with means. The truth is that in the world of business in the next fifty years I doubt that this kind of man will have the breadth of knowledge and wisdom to manage the new mixture of government by business conglomeration. This kind of business executive has been hashed over in hundreds of novels since Sinclair Lewis discovered Babbitt. In 1969, while the Mikes and Babbitts are obviously still very much with us, there is a new breed of man emerging. Amazingly, in business and commerce, too. If you peruse an occasional issue of *Fortune* magazine you will find them. Not hundreds but a few. Top executives who dare to subscribe to and read *The Moscow News* or the *Peking Review* (you can subscribe to them, too). Men who want to compare the political and social input they are receiving from *Time* magazine or *The New York Times* with a direct viewpoint from other cultures. Men who are interested in the whole man and discovering the really avant-garde thinkers like Abraham Maslow, Carl Rogers, Erich Fromm, Rollo May, Herbert Otto, Colin Wilson, George Leonard, and hundreds of others who for the past ten or fifteen years have slowly evolved a new approach to life and to man that already is beginning to infiltrate all major Western religions, and quite possibly in the next hundred years will become a Religion and Philosophy of Man that will be integrated into the whole life plan of man from birth to death.

The real problem for most of us is that we are living through the birth pangs of the new society, and our educational system has failed to give *all* men historical perspective so that they can act effectively to usher the new baby into the world. The Vietnam war, the struggle for Black Power, the student riots, violence and the presumed solutions in law and order, the impact of television, the secularization of the church and synagogue, and the sexual revolution are the direct result of a better educated but still only partially educated population.

The real problem is to try to understand what is happening. Here is part of an editorial from the October 6, 1968, issue of *The Wall Street Journal*.

How strange, too, that the Negroes, who have known actual injustice, are so conspicuously absent from the foul-mouthed little bands pursuing Senator Muskie and Vice President Humphrey. The hecklers are middle-class college students, the ones so splendidly protected from knowledge of real hardship by the American system. Lacking that knowledge, they think they discover hardship wherever they look. If their candidate loses a political battle, the American system is evil and must be destroyed.

These attitudes leave the older generation feeling that life has somehow cheated them. So many of their sons and daughters seem to be fools incapable of distinguishing between Lyndon Johnson and Adolf Hitler; and what is worse, the older generation has a sinking suspicion about why this is so. We recently heard one of them exclaim (implications) "a real depression would be good for this country."

Many middle-aged Americans are likely to feel that youth rebels not because it feels deep grievances but precisely because it has never felt any. What troubles the older generation is the nagging thought that this ill-mannered rebellion is regard not for its failures but its success.

The whole attitude expressed in this editorial is a failure to grasp the larger historical perspective. But it is typical not only of my generation but of many of the younger generation to condemn without analysis. As a contrast read the manifesto of the Midpeninsula Free University, which functions within the environs of Stanford.

We feel that the American educational establishment has proven incapable of meeting the needs of our society. It often discourages students from thinking critically, and does not afford them meaningful training to help them understand the crucial issues confronting mankind today. Bound to the existing power structure, and handicapped by modes of thought fostered by big business, by the military establishment, by consensus politics, and by the mass media, it is unable to consider freely and objectively the cultural, economic, and political forces so rapidly transforming the modern world. The present educational system in fact defends the status quo, perpetuating its evils and perils. The system has become rigid; it is no longer receptive to meaningful change. A revolution in American education is required to meet today's needs, and a new type of education—a free university—must provide the impetus for change.

THEREFORE WE AFFIRM:

That freedom of inquiry is the cornerstone of education.

That each individual must generate his own most vital questions & program his own education, free from central control by administrative bureaucracies and disciplinary oligarchies.

That the class character of age in our society subverts education, and that the young are not too young to teach, nor the old too old to learn.

That education is not a commodity, and should not be measured out in units, grade points, and degrees.

That education is a process involving the total environment, which can only occur in a total community, in which each individual participates equally in making the decisions which importantly affect his life.

That education which has no consequences for social action or personal growth is empty.

That action which does not raise our level of consciousness is futile.

That the ultimate politics will be based on

knowledge, liberty, and community, rather than on hate, fear, or guilt.

That the most revolutionary thing we can do is think for ourselves, and regain contact with our vital centers.

That the most important questions which confront us must be asked again and again, and answered again and again, until the millennium comes.

That the natural state of man is ecstatic wonder.

That we should not settle for less."

Both *The New York Times* editorial and the manifesto of Midpeninsula (incidentally, I think what is going on at Midpeninsula is great and vital) tend to throw the baby out with the bath water. One viewpoint extols the virtues of the past and tries to give the impression we are already living in Utopia, or that at least, with all its faults, this is a pretty damned good world. The other, while affirming positive educational values, excoriates, wanders into anarchy and big-baggage words like "total community" and "ecstatic wonder" with no clear concept of how to bring this new world they have postulated into existence.

5

My feeling is that the small changes and big changes that must come will come from men who have fully grasped the historical continuities. Armed with knowledge, they can then propose new viable answers.

Because I believe with Herbert Otto, who says in his book *A Guide to Developing Your Potential,*

The sexual revolution marks the full scale emergence of a problem which can never be constructively handled as long as it is kept under cover. Man's sexuality and man's potential are intricately and inseparably linked. The current sexual revolution should not be allowed to degenerate into a tug-of-war between the forces of liberalism and those of censorship and repression. It offers us a singular opportunity for self-confrontation and for examining the relationship of man's sexuality with his social institutions and the way these aspects of man's nature can best be shaped to tap his huge potential.

Because I believe this, I began to write and try to express a new kind of sexuality for man based on deep personal interaction between the male and female, not as sexual objects but as human beings. This is a vastly simple idea that has been lost sight of historically. Most of us have never really examined the roots of our Western religious heritage which has perpetuated all of the values and necessities of cultures long forgotten. During the early centuries of man's life on this planet man's prime business was survival. Introspection is not the order of the day when the needs of the body must be met. Hunger and the drive to copulate are prime biological forces that in a hostile world give the male little time for subjectivity. Woman was an object into which he was compelled to eject his seed. Today, thousands of years removed from that primitive creature, man has built his culture and his arts, his religions and his laws, on that subject-object relationship. And even today, for most Western men, whether she is venerated or raped, woman is a sexual object first and a human being second. While some scholars might contest me and cite the strong feminine principle active in some Eastern religions, the fact remains that the I *am* Thou relationship is a philosophy and not a way of life in China, India, or Japan.

With that perspective, it's quite easy to trace the development of our repressed sexuality. The object became property, property produces heirs, and the natural sexual proclivities of the object have to be controlled. Our current sexual revolution is not really a revolution at all. It is simply one phase in the long struggle of the female to free herself from that control and domination. While the current phase has achieved more freedom for the female, she has not escaped the subject-object relationship. In fact, the female has been historically so conditioned that she often has difficulty expressing herself except as an object.

6

So, as a businessman who had shaken off most of his puritanical heritage except the admonition not to waste time (I had succumbed to a slim book by the nearly forgotten novelist Arnold Bennett, *How to Live on Twenty-four Hours a Day*), I decided that instead of ranting to a few friends about the deplorable state of the novel, I would try to write a novel that expressed a different kind of male-female relationship—a merging of the seeming polarity. Not a novel of despair, not a novel that simply mirrored back the author's conception of reality, but rather a warm, loving sexual book about a new kind of hero who refused "to make tragedies where there is no tragedy." In the words of Yale Marratt (and myself),

> Everywhere you turn people or persons fail to measure up to some idiotic idea another person has of himself and boom you have the seeds of self destruction. Look at the world around you. What is the basis of all the hatred but a deluded idea of the importance of self. Look at the murders in the morning paper, the divorces, the man-made scandals. What does it all amount to but a form of ego-mania? a feeling that the *I* is so damned important that it must justify itself at all cost. Do you know, I'll wager ninety-five percent of the novels written or the plays produced each year would have no basis for existence if it weren't for making tragedies where no tragedy should ever exist. There is only one tragedy in the world, and that is this terrible delusion with the importance of self.

After World War II the sex-word revolution in fiction, which began with Norman Mailer finally getting the words fuck and shit into print, was followed by James Jones, whose *From Here to Eternity* completely broke through the dirty word barrier. Of course, Henry Miller, writing in the thirties, had preceded them both, but only tourists to Paris and a few college students had read Olympia Press editions of Miller. The twenty-year flood has finally culminated in whole book stores in our major cities devoted to "fucking literature," and bizarre sex. Why did we extol our popular novelists who were acting like snickering kids who had just discovered how babies were born and were finally getting it printed in books instead of scrawling it on toilet walls? Notice, I use the past tense. Something may have been gained. All the dirty words have been said, all the devalued sex acts have been described, not once but a million times, and the reader who at first was delightfully shocked is now only left with aching eyeballs, boredom, and a realization that after you have covered premarital sex, adultery, lesbianism, homosexualism, transvestism, sodomy, or even cacophagia, the missing ingredient is the *mind* of the man or woman behind the act. Amazingly, most modern novelists, even such a skilled grammarian as John Updike, have failed to give the reader the essential element he wants most: the deep subjective interaction between human beings. Thus sex in a novel like *Couples* is little more than a verbalization of the objective fucking that appears in a daring new eight millimeter movie called *Lovemaking*. Distributed by Grove Press for home viewing, it theoretically offers an artistic expression of the sex act. The only improvement I could see over typical stag films is that it doesn't concentrate on the penis plunging in and out of the vagina. Sadly, while John Updike can revel in lovely word descriptions that make a motion picture pale by comparison, he is still describing the actions of robots. Updike might say, perhaps, they have no brains to begin with, but Yale Marratt would contest him.

With no particular deadline (happily independent of how publishers and editors thought novels should be written), writing in long hand in school notebooks on weekends and on a commuter train that formerly ran between Boston and Quincy, I slowly evolved a character who was me and not me. He would personify two words that most novelists in the period 1962-64 had forgotten. Rebellion and Challenge. I was convinced that the typical popular novelist portraying the dregs of society and the lunatic fringe was trying to endow the actions of an unhealthy minority with some kind of insane validity for man as a whole. What the novel needed was modern heroes. Instead, the reader was being engulfed by writers and critics in a great literary put-on. We were being sold heroes and heroines like those who appear in *Valley of the Dolls, The Group, The Chapman Report, The Voyeur, Portnoy's Complaint*: men and women caught up in a morass of sexual problems and sexual neuroses. Sick people whose only concept of love is self-love, jealousy, possessiveness, or the pursuit of fame. If that were not sufficient even the venerable *New York Times* succumbed to critics who tried to convince us that *The Story of O* is a great revelation of female masochism, or that *Candy* is really a sly poke at pornography, or that *The Last Exit to Brooklyn* reveals the essence of the ghetto. Our new heroes were trapped in the degraded sexuality of *The Arrangement*, or were nymphet lovers of Lolitas, or were having hundred dollar misunderstandings with erotic black girls, or, on a lesser plane, were James Bonds (bedside reading of a former President of the United States) whose main sexual characteristic could be summed up in the little poem, "He fucked and ran away so he could live to fuck another day."

Horribly, our sexual revolution is making us bolder

sexually, but we are still afraid of warm, loving, sentient, erotic sex. Females are still objects. Unable to reveal our sexual potential in the written word, where at least the possibility exists of subjective portrayal (if we could escape our cultural conditioning), we are now experiencing the group-grope of the even more difficult subjective art of the moving picture film.

On October 13, 1968, Renata Adler, then film critic for *The New York Times*, stops to wonder:

I don't know quite what to make of this, and perhaps it is only a reaction to the days when stars were blown up as love goddesses, but it is really startling what cinema, particularly American cinema, has done in the past year or so to women. With few exceptions (Virginia Maskell in "Interlude," Maggie Smith in "Hot Millions," Estelle Parsons and Joanne Woodward in "Rachel, Rachel," and even these were actresses whose personal humanity overcame their roles), they have been grotesques—kooks, vampires, murderesses, spies, careerists, lesbians, objects of torture, torturers, nymphomaniacs or warmhearted, one-dimensional vulgarisms that pass for somebody's idea of what a Jewish mother is. What makes me think about it now, although it has been in the air these many months, is "Barbarella"—a movie so dead, humorless and puerile that it would not quite have made the grade as a fifties college musical, a movie that includes, among other over-rated writers of our time, the author of "Candy", and which suggests, almost incidentally, that some of the least imaginative minds of our generation, except for Beckett, Donleavy, Barthelme, are going the farthest out.

Really, viewed in a larger perspective our sex confusion is kind of funny-sad!

Because I believe in a world where casually accepted nudity would help resolve some of our sexual repressions, years ago I contacted the American Sunbathing Association. While I believe in being naked when it's convenient, I could never be bothered driving hundreds of miles to walk around naked with people whose only common interest was being undressed. For many years (needing the reinforcement of knowing that I was not alone) I subscribed to their publications. Ten years ago, nudists believed the only way to spread their philosophy was through magazines showing family-togetherness naked. They were bugged by the fact that the laws required them to airbrush the genitals and pubic hairs on all such publications. A few years ago they finally won a Supreme Court case to the effect that photographic depiction of the human body with the genital organs was not indecent. They were about to reap the whirlwind! It sealed the doom of the old-fashioned nudist magazines.

If at last genitals weren't indecent, enterprising publishers of girlie magazines knew where the *real* demand lay. In the vernacular of the trade, let's really have "split-beaver shots." It's a sad fact most men never get to see the female with her legs spread. All the nudists had wanted to accomplish was to show the female delta and the male penis, with pubic hairs. I'm sure they never suspected they would be responsible for entire magazines, devoted to lovely white and black girls inviting you to examine their entire bush, labia majora, labia minora, and, for good measure (in some camera angles), their pulsating anus. Females are still objects. Maybe the poor male really wants to crawl back into the gaping hole and escape forever into the fluid womb.

It's sad because this new phase of the sexual revolution might have been avoided if the historical cultural conditioning of Western man hadn't pierced into the very marrow of his morality. I'm grinning! I really don't think this stage of the cure is worse than the disease! Perhaps we'll have to go the whole way. We already have a quickie underground cinema industry devoted wholly to sex that proceeds, de Sade fashion, into mutilation of the female to create the ultimate orgasmic situation. Linking sex with violence has already emerged into the legitimate cinema in *Rosemary's Baby* and *Bonnie and Clyde*, to mention a few of our so called top-drawer movies.

While our critics tell us that this is great stuff, I believe that just below the surface a counterrevolution is in the making. When it comes we won't need the nude girlie magazines or the *Playboy* gatefolds, because we will be living in a world where the males see females (and vice versa) running, jumping, playing as naked, living human beings. The counterrevolution is quietly saying that human beings in this society are using only a tenth of their potential. The missing ninety percent includes their potential as completely expressed sexual creatures.

7

Is sex finished in the novel and the cinema? Of course not! Not if we get a grip on ourselves and don't go the way of Huxley's *Brave New World*, allowing ourselves to be produced artificially in incubators. What is finished is strictly genital sex without love. (Lest I be accused of using a big-baggage word like "love" I won't define it here.) In *Harrad*, *Yale Marratt*, and *Proposition 31*, I've tried to make the intangible tangible. But so far as most of the current novelists go, they have exhausted objective sex. Now they are only repeating themselves. They have portrayed man and woman at such a low level of thinking existence, with such a small use of the gift of their minds divorced from their genital reactions, that all they have succeeded in doing is creating a picture of man as basically depraved, immoral, and ugly. They have carried the thunder of the prophets of the New Testament and the founders of Judaism and Christianity (remember, Jesus didn't invent Christianity) to it's inevitable absurdity. If man is really like our novelists and film writers have been saying, we better explode the nuclear weapons now. "Let's all go together when we go . . . in a nice incandescent glow."

If you believe that the typical writer today is giving you a true vision of man, if you believe you can point up similarities in your own environment, in your own personal lives, you are only partially right. The missing element in these books and moving pictures is that by your own essence as a male or female you can't escape your own humanity. *You are not ultimately evil!* There is no true dichotomy that can be labeled good and evil in man. Despite writers like Lorenz and Ardrey who try to overwhelm you with concepts about aggression and the territorial imperative, who tell you that this is the reason you are what you are, you *know* deep down they are wrong. Man is good or evil as he is reinforced for good or evil by his environment. And environment is very largely a man-created product that can be changed!

You, the youngsters who detected the hypocrisy in politics, you the young radicals who are demanding a new kind of honesty from the older generation, should demand the same kind of art from your writers, poets, artists, and musicians. Not tell it like it is. Tell it like it *can* be, and *we* will make it that way.

No, sex is not washed up in fiction . . . nor in life. What

we need now are novelists who are really trying to understand man. Every once in a while a moving picture appears like *The Two of Us* or *Closely Watched Trains* (sadly, this kind of achievement is more prevalent in the foreign cinema than in Hollywood productions or in the novel), and I cheer to see the younger generation jamming the theaters. This is the kind of writing and film we desperately need. Writers of this kind fill a basic need. They are creating modern heroes. The reading and viewing public are hungry for them. They need them in their lives to reinforce the deep down humanness which a former generation raised on outmoded Freudian concepts has been afraid to expose to the sunlight. Heroes who can triumph over man-made problems. Not men and women who are sucked into the whirlpool of sexual depravity and despair, and from this vantage point insist that the rest of the world is like them. They remind me of that old cartoon they used to hang in lavatories. The tramp is immersed in the toilet bowl and is about to flush himself down. "Good-bye cruel world!"

It is interesting to note that several years ago the need for some kind of hero created a resurgence of the TV Western and a revival of Humphrey Bogart movies. Here at least were men who triumphed over evil. Men who had no doubts. But these heroes were one dimensional. The modern hero should have plenty of doubts, plenty of fears, but he should persist against them. The writers the world needs are the writers who will give us the feeling that the hero will more than persist—*he will triumph because of his own inner strengths.* We need novelists who will portray little men who become big people. Not materialistically big people—God no!—but little people who refuse to wallow in the mire of their petty jealousies and hatreds.

So the first novel I attempted was *The Rebellion of Yale Marratt.* What about Yale Marratt and his rebellion? Isn't rebellion a lovely word in this world of conformism? It is characterized by a lack of fear of change. Most people past thirty are scared to death of change, and *that* is the generation gap. Rebellion is even a better word with a thinking brain behind it. Not rebellion for rebellion's sake, but a rebellion that knows where it is going. Not just an adolescent rebellion against authority, but a rebellion against a world of laws, religions, jealousies, prejudices, and hatreds that have made a mulligan stew out of man's finest feelings and emotions. A rebellion against a world

26

that gives lip service to the idea that it is man's mission to make tragedies where no tragedy should exist.

The essence of Yale's rebellion is summed up in the ten commandments of Challenge. They are scattered throughout the book. But for hundreds who have asked me, here they are in one place.

1. Challenge believes that Man is God.
2. Challenge believes that men must be taught to challenge and excoriate any concepts that deny the ultimate divinity of Man.
3. Challenge is not concerned with the immortality of Man. Man must be taught to seek his salvation on this earth and in this lifetime through the Love and Understanding of all men.
4. Challenge believes that the only destiny of Man is the pursuit of knowledge, and every Man of sound mind and body should actively pursue his destiny.
5. Challenge believes that no Man is preconditioned to act by metaphysical fate or man-conceived determinism.
6. Challenge believes that Man is the measure of all ethical and moral values, and the test of validity in Man's ethics and morals and written laws should be that they exalt and confirm the dignity of Man.
7. Challenge believes that any human problem (hence, all problems known to Man) can be solved in the atmosphere of Love, and that the existence of hate as an emotion should be extirpated from Man's relationships and be considered the greatest evil confronting civilization.
8. Challenge believes that in the sexual union of Man and Woman, all men, regardless of language, race, or creed, become deeply aware of the Beauty and Goodness inherent in each Man and Woman, and that through proper instruction from childhood can learn to transfer this Ultimate Insight into their daily commerce with each other.
9. Challenge believes that its beliefs are so honestly right for today's civilization that if men everywhere would accept them and teach them to their children for several generations, eventually a crusade would result that would wipe tyranny and oppression from this world.
10. Challenge will never cease to challenge. No thing . . . no belief, not even the Commandments of Challenge are sacred or inviolable.

Perhaps the last commandment of Challenge is the most important. As a good example, if I were rewriting *Yale Marratt* I would eliminate the word crusade from the ninth commandment. It's not only an ugly word, but we won't change the world with a crusade!

Without trying to summarize the story of Yale Marratt, who ends up married to two women, let me grin a little and tell you that many people consider me a shocking writer. The shock is not from the sexual descriptions in my books, but rather that in all five of them what is normally considered "sin" against the current mores never reverberates on the characters. They all end up living happily in "sin." The ten commandments are but one example. Most modern novelists of the type I have described, if they had a hero married to two women would make an earth shaking, Peyton Place mess out of this situation. Maybe they'd have Yale Marratt shoot himself. After all, living with two women could get sticky. More likely they would have one of the girls still loving Yale, get a divorce, and tearfully bow out. Or if they were influenced by the Victorian tradition, one of the girls, convinced she was the least loved, would commit suicide or maybe be done away with in a convenient automobile accident. *But life isn't that easy.* Moreover, despite all snickerers to the contrary, it *is possible* for three people to love each other. If they are happy to live together, happy to work out their problems ..., if they refuse to make a tragedy out of their mutual love, don't they assume a kind of heroic stance that is completely missing in modern fiction? They become fictional characters worth emulating.

Do I personally believe in bigamy? Yes and no. I do not believe in a bigamy of enslavement, or a situation in which one of the partners involved does not know of the existence of the other. I do believe a bigamous relationship of *three* responsible people ... intelligent people, should be made possible under the laws of the United States. Let me underline *responsible*. In my novel *Proposition 31* I proposed a law which would make possible a legal form of marriage for up to three couples. In *Yale Marratt, Harrad,* and *Proposition 31* there is *structure.* I believe that an approved premarital or postmarital social structure is a necessity not only so individuals can realize themselves fully without guilt feelings but also for the preservation of the family structure. Many people who hear about the mad proposals of Bob

Rimmer feel that I am trying to undermine the family structure of this country. Far from it! I believe that strong family structure is a *sine qua non* of social existence. The trouble with the majority of homes in the United States today is that they are not families ... simply households sustained, in the vast majority of cases, by not more than a total of three or four people including parents and children. No man is an island meant to live alone, and these nuclear households are little better than islands.

So, *Yale Marratt* proposes that for some men and women a *ménage à trois*, existing in the framework of intelligent love, approved by society, would expand their horizons as individuals, and for many women in later life fill out the vacuum of living lonely, boring days in our surburban wastelands. Man and woman can love more than each other. A marriage of three people or of two or three couples could be a lively, exciting business. All it takes is men and women who are willing to use the vast potential of their brains to reexamine the trivia of their man-made emotions.

8

There are several stages to writing a first novel. In the first stage you wonder if you'll ever get it completed, and as you work you tell yourself it doesn't matter, you are really writing it for yourself. If the ignorant world out there rejects you, so much the worse for them. The second stage is when you finally get it completed. Basically, you have to admit you wrote it with the hope someone would read it, but you suddenly realize you have what one writer has called a "white elephant." Since there are some fifty thousand other white elephants continuously circulating among publishers (and who in hell wants a white elephant anyway), the best thing is to console yourself; not every one owns a white elephant! Being a man who believes in rushing in where angels fear to tread, without an agent, I sent *Yale Marratt*, either in its full, bulky form of 750 typewritten pages or as a synopsis, to a total of fourteen publishers who coolly rejected it one after the other. The major complaint of the few who read it (most publishers don't even read unsolicited manuscripts) was that bigamy was a very distasteful subject to females, who read most of the novels. Females read novels to escape and find romance and not be pounded on the head by some guy with a mad thesis that a man could love two women. Worse, their husbands might applaud the whole distasteful

29

idea. Surprisingly, that's not true. It's the husbands who object! Since *Yale Marratt*'s publication, many females have written me that they think it's a great idea—just so long as I agree it might also work in reverse.

After two years of rejections (I even paid a well-known literary agent to read *Yale Marratt*, little realizing he had written a book of advice to writers that included the dictum never to write about bigamy) I decided that if I couldn't change the world with *Yale Marratt*, perhaps I might shock it into a little sexual sanity. Could I write a novel that didn't read like a history swiped from a casebook on psychoanalysis, a book that didn't have one sadistic or masochistic scene in it? Sex that was not degraded or evil . . . but just was. Human sex. Sex with laughter. Laughter not at someone else's expense, but the characters themselves simply enjoying their own healthy sexuality. Willa Starch, the heroine of *That Girl from Boston*, presumably writes the book in the first person and even gets an enema administered by her boyfriend. Later she points out that while this may not be the proper subject for fiction, it certainly is healthier than rape, murder, perversion, and infidelity for the hell of it—subjects which most modern novelists seem enamored of.

1960, when I finished *That Girl from Boston*, was the year before Barney Rossett had convinced the Supreme Court that *Lady Chatterley* was literature and not obscenity. It would be another year before Henry Miller was finally published by Grove Press. Five publishers in rapid succession rejected *That Girl* because people couldn't talk like that in fiction. Grove Press might have wanted to take on the world, but not the more conservative publishers I had solicited. I didn't send the book to Grove Press. Even today, Barney Rossett, who can be hailed as the man who broke through the censorship barriers, still is preoccupied with the nitty-gritty kind of sex book that used to be the stock-in-trade of Maurice Girodias and Olympia Press. Sex as Bob Rimmer writes it is too happy for Grove Press.

I suppose I should have given up. If I hadn't read all those Horatio Alger books I might have. I let the vice-president of the company I run read *That Girl*. He thought it was fun. He had formerly been a managing editor of *Hunting and Fishing* magazine. Admittedly, we didn't know the first thing about publishing and distributing books, but if we could do it as a left-hand, after-hours operation, why not publish it? Babes in the woods. With eight thousand dollars we scraped together (cold analysis shows that it takes at least a half million dollars to get a new book publisher off the ground), we named our publishing company ... what else? Challenge Press! Amazingly, despite newspapers that refused our Sex-With-Laughter advertising, we sold five thousand copies of *That Girl* in a hardcover edition and got delusions of grandeur. Why not incorporate Challenge Press, sell stock, and publish *Yale Marratt* as well as a couple of other books? One thing you'll soon discover if you start a publishing company—you will be deluged with manuscripts. We chose two others: *Some of My Best Friends Are People* by Art Moger and *Cocktail Party for the Author* by Alex Jackinson. My contribution to the new company was irrevocable rights to and all income from *That Girl* and *Yale Marratt*. In exchange I received three hundred shares of stock.

If you are bored in this world, one way to become happily dizzy is to involve yourself in several odd-ball projects. I was running a business, writing *The Harrad Experiment*, and entertaining daydreams of at last discovering a pipeline into the Establishment that I could use to pump in some adrenalin. In essence ... the Establishment didn't respond. Challenge Press became an accumulation of some twenty small stockholders with a maximum wealth of about nineteen thousand dollars. It was too late to withdraw. All three books were in type. We went ahead with the printing and in October of 1964 were the proud owners of 21,000 books (7,000 of each title), and no money to advertise them and no salesmen to sell them. Challenge Press no longer exists. Most of the inventory was sold to overstock booksellers for fifteen cents a copy. I still have about five hundred copies of the original hardcover $6.95 edition of *Yale Marratt*. If you'd like a copy, drop me a note and I'll send you one with my compliments while they last!

9

So much for autobiography. The point is not that we failed ... but that we dared to try. Six months later I had finished *The Harrad Experiment* and I was now the proud owner of three white elephants ... two published, which very few people had read, and one in manuscript ... which was being rapidly rejected by publishers. And then the amazing thing happened. A small West Coast publisher who was making a profitable thing out of publishing and selling by mail just the kind of sex literature I was fulminating against offered a thousand-dollar advance for *The Harrad Experiment*. A forty-page Introduction that was in the original manuscript would have to go, but after some hot argument and an attempt to change some of the approach, it was agreed the basic book would remain as I had written it. Since this company distributed and sold books largely by mail (I didn't know anything about the publisher until the contract was signed), the advertising approach would be left to them.

For hundreds who have written me and asked, let me say that most authors have absolutely no control over the way a book is advertised or the kind of dust jacket or cover that appears on it—a battle I have lost right down to the hardcover edition of *Proposition 31*, with its dust jacket featuring a naked female as "object" (whom I'd like to hug, but who has no similarity to the females in the book).

Now if you read *Harrad*, hold your breath! Here are some excerpts from the four-page mail-order advertising of the hardcover edition:

An Explosive New Sexual Coup d'Etat . . . new erotic thrills . . . shocking sexual abandonment, wild sexual experiment. Sex acts performed by couples, threesomes and circuses! Group sex and every other variation of the sex act comes vibrantly, erotically to life in this daringly unique book. Discover what happens when Sheila Grove and her date from Harrad bring their own ideas about sex to a wild weekend spree at a neighboring college. Sheila winds up in bed and confesses in her diary: "I never imagined what sizes a man could grow to. I held him hard and felt him move against my fingers. ..." In his own words, Harry Schacht tells of his first time with Beth Hillyer . . . as nakedly they writhe together in a huge pile of leaves . . . "the leaves crumbled, turning her white breasts dusty brown. She carefully picked the leaves off my penis." And then moments later "I could feel the soft, undulating movements of her vagina keeping me happily within her."

Discover the candor of the scene where Beth poses nude for a center-spread in *Cool Boy Magazine*— while her five friends look on, also completely nude! Beth goes with Harry into the bathroom where, sprawled on the floor together, he shaves her intimately in preparation for the photography session.

And then there are the private experiments as different couples develop ways of prolonging the sex act:

STANLEY AND SHEILA (from both of their diaries)

Stanley says to Sheila: *"When I kiss you like that I can feel your vagina contract on me,"* And Sheila writes in her own diary: *"Stanley was kissing me between the legs. 'You taste quite nice,' he said."*

HARRY AND VALERIE (from Harry's diary)

Harry describes the orgiastic aftermath of a beach party on Cape Cod: *"Val was holding my penis lightly. . . . Our climax was hungrily joyful."*

JACK AND BETH (from Beth's diary)

Beth confronts Jack, saying: *". . . I've made love with three different Harrad boys. You've only made love with me."*
Jack replies: *"I'm happy. Besides, we've got three years to go." "While this conversation was going on Jack had undressed. I followed him into the bedroom. . ."*

You'll also read of the nude wrestling matches where the girls take on the boys! And there's the time Beth and Stanley arrive early at the hotel suite the six have reserved for a wild New Year's Eve party. They are discovered in bed together by the others who take immediate action to ensure their own good time! You'll read of the abandoned nude dancing at Bad Max's bar in Greenwich Village! And who hungers after Sheila's ripe body! There's Asoka, the tempting 15-year-old prostitute from India who Stanley finds in his bed! You'll enjoy all the wildness of making an "experimental" movie which ends in a mass raid and jail for the six Harrad students on vice charges! And after college, there is the communal living, the willing sharing of bodies that leads Valerie to remark: *"Every Sunday when my new husband for the week joins me, I feel like a new bride again!"*

When I first read this advertising (more than a half

million pieces were finally mailed), I didn't know whether to laugh or cry. So I laughed. I *now knew* why my original Introduction to *Harrad* had been cut to six pages. Every approach to sex and love that I had excoriated (not very subtly) both in the book and in the Introduction was *being used to sell "The Harrad Experiment."** It's an interesting commentary on most of the past-thirty generation that there is only one kind of sex in the world. They are victims of their Christian-Judaistic heritage. Sex is dirty and that's all there is to it! Of course, the publisher knew his mail-order market ... all men, well past thirty! I often wonder what the reactions were of the eighteen thousand of them who bought the hardcover edition of *Harrad* by mail. It was published in April of 1966 and I never received a letter from any of them pro or con!

10

So *Harrad* is your book! When the Bantam edition was published in February of 1967 (with the female lamb being led to the slaughter on the cover ... and the blurb "The Sex Manifesto of the Free Love Generation"—not the author's idea of any female in the book, and very definitely not "free love"), you told each other and millions of you bought it, and *you* understood what I was trying to say! At the grim old age of forty-eight, Bob Rimmer was finally no longer a reverse kind of Minniver Cheevy born too early and assailing the seasons. The people I believed in, the new generation who were questioning every value my generation had lived by and calling the shots where they fall, has overwhelmingly said Yes ... "we believe in what you are saying." Because of you, *Yale Marratt* was finally published in paperback. Because of you *The Zolotov Affair*, which I wrote *after Harrad*, was bought by publishers who hated it. Perhaps you too wonder about *Zolotov* ... but if you read it carefully you'll discover that Horace Zolotov, who turns lead into gold in his basement (with Marge Wentworth along for the ride) is tackling the outmoded economic values in an attempt to warn you against the politicians who would rather go down in one big economic bust than create a world where money does what it's supposed to do—simplify the exchange of goods between men, whose prime purpose is living, not self-aggrandizement.

*Thanks to The New American Library, the missing portion of the Introduction was restored in the British edition of the book published by The New English Library.

But let me warn you. Read the last commandment of Challenge again. I don't believe in people who come waving a flag and say, "Follow me. My way is the way. I have the pure vision." I *am not* in a lesser way an Ayn Rand inviting you to the holy tabernacle of objectivism or a Ron Hubbard running courses in my pure conception of Scientology. I'm not like Mary Baker Eddy excising her foot-noted debt to Hindu philosophy from the first edition of *Science and Health, with a Key to the Scriptures.* Rather, I am a simple person like you at the confluence of history. To the shock of my publishers I put bibliographies in my novels, not to show my erudition, but to tell you I am derivative. What I am writing in the form of novels, trying to show you in practice, is being said and written in hundreds of outposts in this country.

When a group in Boston asked if I would object if they published a newsletter called *The Harrad Letter,* * I told them to go ahead. Not because this would be a vehicle to put across the message of Bob Rimmer (I have no connection with the publisher), but rather to give you confidence that you are not alone in this world. If you wish to join societies for the propagation of this or that, it's all right with me. If you wish to live my way, I think we'll move things faster. Be a gadfly to the world and yourself. Learn how to live in the world and manipulate *in it, and out of it,* and as you refuel in the out-phase you'll discover *your* way to change it. Question everything ... *but not to destroy the world.* Question everything to understand the world and yourself better!

So let's question *Harrad* and *Proposition 31.* Are they feasible proposals? Could they work in practice or are they the Pollyanna vision of some kind of out-of-this-world character who believes that people can really learn to love each other and be defenseless with each other?

First let me digress to throw some sidelights on the *Harrad* and *Proposition 31* proposals. In his latest book, *The Revolution of Hope,* Erich Fromm has sounded a call to action to create a new, humanized technology. I urge you to read this book concurrently with George Leonard's *Education and Ecstasy* and Herbert Otto's *Guide to Developing Your Potential.* If I were functioning as a Phillip Tenhausen, early in the freshman phase of the

*For a free copy of *The Harrad Letter* and subscription information write H. Randall Webb, 145 Walden Street, Cambridge, Massachusetts.

seminar on Human Values at Harrad College, I would incorporate all three books. These men are vanguard thinkers pointing directly to the way the winds of the future must blow. Since the entire direction of the Human Values course as I have proposed it in *The Harrad Experiment* would be to answer the question of whether or not there are basic values, almost in the sense of natural law, I want to emphasize that the "encounter" nature of such a continuing seminar would be a freewheeling interaction between the husband and wife team as leaders and the students. This four-year approach could well become the most significant part of the undergraduate educational experience. Evaluation and correlation of the entire day-to-day learning experience in the various studies being pursued by the students would be in the framework of core values evolved by the participating students and the leaders. Since the seminar would be a continuous learning experience and not indoctrination or brainwashing, the leaders themselves would become students in the exciting and challenging interaction. Boredom would vanish as learning became an exciting and ecstatic participation in the now-world emerging from the past-world.

A basic premise of *Harrad, Yale Marratt*, and *Proposition 31* is that any continuing group experience—whether it be temporary groups such as sensitivity-training labs or structured or unstructured encounter groups—requires a goal-directed male and female participation and a life-seeking purpose on which the participants agree. With this approach the Human Values seminar, which should be evolved in groups of not more than ten couples, would have constant input and avoid the tendency of groups to navel contemplation. If the initial class of freshmen were fifty couples, five separate groups could meet together once a week and compare their thinking. The overriding effect of such a continuing seminar throughout the college experience would be self-stimulating curiosity, drive, and interest. I use "interest" in the same sense as Erich Fromm does in *Revolution and Hope*. "Interest comes from the Latin *inter-esse*, that is 'to be in-between.' If I am interested I must transcend my ego, be open to the world, jump into it. Interest is based on activeness."

I am not acquainted with George Leonard or Erich Fromm except through their books, but I am sure that we all agree the new world we are envisioning must be achieved by a vastly different approach to education than now exists in our society. Both Fromm and Leonard (and many other educators) are asking for a world where lifelong learning, and in the process constantly evaluated and reevaluated experience of the present and the past (we, as human beings in historical time), is a self-impelled driving force of man.

The other premise of *Harrad* and *Proposition 31*, that males and females become co-disciples in the learning process and live together as roommates, shocks those who have been conditioned that the male and female should restrain their sexuality during the undergraduate learning process. While the concept of separated educational facilities for males and females has only a few outposts left, the merger of formerly all-male institutions with all-female institutions, and our coed state universities (most of which still maintain sharp dormitory divisions), are a far cry from the *Harrad* proposal. Here is an amusing Associated Press dispatch of Temple University's experience with a closer living association of males and females.

Temple University is calling off its experiment of mixing the sexes in a previously all-male dorm.

It just didn't work out.

During the past school year, 42 girls were programmed, because of overcrowding, to share Johnson Hall, a dorm for 300 men. When classes resume in September, there won't be any such sharing.

"Sex wasn't the problem," Mrs. Jan Austin, girls' dorm boss who tried to make it work, said today. "It was the sexes. They just couldn't function as an organized dorm unit."

The students couldn't agree on how to govern themselves, how to hand out discipline, and they had trouble discussing personal problems together. Even dating flopped.

"They reacted as brothers and sisters to each other," Mrs. Austin said.

A survey before the term-end splitup showed even in complaints on dorm living there is a difference between men and women.

The girls wanted private showers, a quiet lounge, more closet space. The boys, happy to shower together, beefed about laundry, closed lounges, and rules keeping women out of their rooms.

Does this Temple experience indicate that a Harrad

type living program would come apart at the seams? I honestly don't think so. Permitting males and females in the same dormitory *is not putting an individual male and female in the same room*, and just as important, it is not giving them the correlation and reinforcement of the Human Values Seminar. Nor is it exposing them to the continuing sharing and the deeper emotional experience of a male and female with the leaders (the Tenhausens or their equivalent) as well as with their peer group, or the academic pressure to obtain their undergraduate degrees. A Harrad type program would humanize the entire educational environment and restore the driving curiosity, wonder, and commitment to learning as a lifelong process.

11

One vital aspect of the learning experience which even Leonard omits in his book *Education and Ecstasy* is that the sheer joy of learning "the positive reinforcement" (in the words of B. F. Skinner), is the *shared* learning experience. The college grind (they called them "greasy grinds" in my college days), getting all A's and ultimately his Phi Beta Kappa key, is often dehumanized by his simple inability to share with his peer group. Granted that sharing (as simple as two people, or a group, reacting *together* to the "discovery" of music, art, or some writer on the same wave length) can exist in a male to male relationship. But the ecstatic experience is male and female minds, with their inevitably different biological conditionings, catalyzing each other and discovering that the *I am Thou* experience *can be learned* as a process of interacting growth. In bed, sexually joined, too! I chuckle at comments on my books that I am guilty of writing some of the longest sexual encounters in fiction. My characters presumably talk too much as they make love. Probing minds, trying to find the words to discover themselves and their ecstasy (despite Esalen and the new emphasis on nonverbal communication), is still the only final way of deep communication between human beings. The trouble is that most people not only do not dare to try to say the words that would reveal their humanity but they do not know how to listen and revel in the other person's humanity without casting judgment. After four years of a Harrad type seminar the *how* of verbal communication would be second nature to the participants.

If we are ever to achieve a creative kind of sexuality and love experience in this society, a valid starting point would be to pass laws which would make possible, within the framework of *socially approved* mores, a premarital experience similar to Harrad, a time in a male and female's life when monogamous marriage was not specifically formalized. What better time is there than in the undergraduate years? During this phase of their lives males and females could discover themselves both as sexual human beings and as persons, expanding their awareness of themselves in the ongoing part of the education process. I have suggested as a total social concept that individuals who passed through the Harrad experience would in most cases function monogamously during the early child-bearing years, and then after the couple had passed the age of thirty, *if they wished* they could take advantage of a socially approved form of marriage of two couples, combining their lives into a corporate family.

I am amused when people object to these ideas on the basis that I am proselytizing for this kind of premarital and postmarital experience as a way of life for everybody. *Now*, in the year 1969, I definitely don't believe that Harrad, or corporate marriage, or bigamous marriage is for everybody. I am simply saying that since we permit the existence of bachelors, spinsters (and should permit the existence of economic dropouts, whether they be priests, rabbis, ministers, or hippies), we should in a vital democracy also permit alternative marriage or premarital arrangements. The central concept of any society should be the preservation of a healthy family system—family structures, whether they be monogamous, corporate, or bigamous, that can give children security and the ability to cope with a technological age. If such laws existed, a college of the Harrad type starting today would be for the few, just as corporate marriages would be for those who were certain they were emotionally and intellectually ready for it. Obviously, a later courtship of two couples might take several years before it was consummated in corporate marriage. But if a Harrad type program could be started now within the framework of one of the larger universities, I not only feel they would have no trouble getting applicants (parentally approved) but that in ten years the idea would spread to such an extent that every major university and college would offer similar programs. The end result in twenty-five to fifty years would be several hundred thousand males and females, an emotional and intellectual élite, who could charter this country on an exciting new voyage into a world where the day-to-day business of living was an exciting adventure in self-actualization and self-discovery.

Every day we are getting closer to the inevitability of this type of education. We no longer seriously believe that somehow two relative strangers, a male and female, with different family backgrounds, with different value approaches to life, and often with very different sexual conditioning received from their parents and the church, after a few months or even a year of "discovering" each other (the engagement) can marry into a sweet, everlasting monogamous heaven until they die. We live in a sex-tease society where the female is blatantly promoted as a romantic object that no male can live without, and the male is conceived of as a somewhat stupid character designed for the purpose of impregnating the female. Analyze the large circulation of ladies' magazines and see if this isn't one basic concept. To counterbalance it we have freely available pornography (conceived by frustrated males, obviously). Here the male is in such powerful phallic control that he not only assuages his desires but usually ends up mutilating the female who, quite untrue to life, is a masochist and keeps coming back for more. With this kind of preconditioning if you believe that somehow the male and female, finally safely married, can blunder through into a happy acceptance of each other as human beings with only their immediate family, or religious counselors, or some doctor (often as hung up as his patient) or the mass media and rudimentary courses in sex education in high school or college to guide them in the vast potential of human relationships; if you believe that a female who offers a man as her greatest gift premarital chastity and the inexperience of a virgin bride, then you believe in miracles.

A few weeks ago I was the guest of a popular local, late-evening radio telephone show. One lady after listening to me expound the premise of Harrad told me I made her so nervous at the sheer insanity of the idea that she had left her bed (beside her presumably sleeping husband, since it was one o'clock in the morning) and was tossing restlessly about on her living room floor in desperate fear that her daughter might read such a flagrant book as *The Harrad Experiment*. Another listener (a female) drew me into an extended discussion on the age the young male achieved the height of his sexual virility. I told her I would guess approximately at the age of eighteen or nineteen. Triumphantly she pointed out the obvious

40

conclusion—a male living with a female would probably rape her the first night.

It constantly amazes me that the older generation has so thoroughly forgotten their youthful idealism. The moment you suggest a male and female living together unmarried, the concomitant vision is lust, orgies, alcohol, pot smoking, or, at the very least, the poor female suffering because of her greater love and ultimate rejection by the male. Unquestionably, at the beginning some Harrad students would be dissatisfied with their roommates, but based on a careful preselection program, I'm certain it would be a great deal fewer than would be anticipated. Keep in mind this is not a marriage. The roommates do not have to sleep together. It is also assumed they would shift roommates. The assignment of roommates would not only have to take into account the mental and emotional background of the males and females who would room together, but it would obviously have to relate to the popular concepts of male and female "beauty." Thus, it would be impractical to choose roommates who deviated too sharply from the norms.

By this I do not mean racial homogeneity, but rather reasonable standards of weight and physical health. Obviously, if a dormitory living program of the Harrad style was functioning, black students should be admitted. While this may be more shocking to some of the black and white community than the idea of a structured experimental premarital environment, I am convinced that all the elements of black separatism, including black studies programs just for blacks (the whites need them more!), are only temporary solutions for the black people in their search for identity. We must ultimately create a society where white or black racists recognize the complete stupidity of their attitudes: a society where black and white are human beings first, and only incidentally of different skin colors. A premarital living program embracing a percentage of black male and female students who were accepted as freshmen would, in the second or third years, create an atmosphere where some black and white males and females would room with a student of the opposite sex and race. With the rapidly developing higher emotional and intellectual level of Harrad students, I would predict that by their junior year most Harrad students would have encountered a member of the opposite race not only sexually but with an involvement and commitment that for some would lead to interracial marriage. At the very least, a Harrad environment would

41

bring black and white students together in a close emotional and intellectual camaraderie that does not exist to any degree in the typical college or university today.

One of the joys of the letters that I continually receive from readers is the utter impossibility of dogmatically answering all the pros and cons raised. Some readers do not like the idea of prestructuring the roommate system at Harrad. Let us find our own boyfriend or girlfriend and proceed from there. All right, why not? But can you avoid rooming with your own choice of roommates during the entire four years? My feeling is that Harrad shouldn't simply duplicate the typical "going steady" premarital environment with the additional feature of permissive sex contacts. The four years at Harrad should be a time for each student to discover at least three or four members of the opposite sex in depth, with the dawning realization that sex separated from deep subjective involvement quickly becomes devalued currency. The ultimate monogamous choice will come between people who "need" each other, who reinforce each other on multiple levels as complete human beings.

Many readers have taken apart the proposal for a take-over of the State X (incidentally, for those who have asked, the possible states I had in mind were Montana, Wyoming, or North Dakota) and I cheer them. While the proposal is considerably more Utopian in concept than the establishment of a Harrad College, it has the merit of asking the key question and seeking the specific answers. If we are rebelling against the system as it now is ... what kind of society do we want to achieve? One thing should be apparent; we can no longer afford the luxury of democratic drift. Unlike past generations, we *must* attempt to plan the future and in the process predicate a government which is still democratically oriented but, as Gore Vidal has suggested, has an area of agreed upon social priorities that must be achieved and are not subject to the changing winds of federal or state politics. If I were to write the proposal for a take-over of a state in detail, reshaping it to answer human needs, quite obviously there would be hundreds of points of conflict with both the older generation and the younger generation. Good! The best of Utopianists gets caught up in his own ego ideals. But (and it's been said before) it's getting too late in man's history on this planet to think of anything less than

Utopias. We won't achieve them anyway . . . but in the process may emerge a value structure that millions can agree on.

Quite a few readers of *Harrad* have objected to the Phi Beta Kappa level of the students. Is this a criterion? Good lord, no! I'm chuckling as I write this. Based on my own background, if all-around top grades were a requisite for admission, I would never have been accepted to Harrad! Much more important as an overall guide for selection would be males and females who come from a liberal background and who have shown in some areas a drive to learn or have revealed in their approach to life an untapped creative potential—young males and females who at the age of seventeen or eighteen have not been brainwashed by their families or the culture and still retain a high sense of curiosity and childhood wonder and discontent with the status quo. Since the Harrad experience would in a sense be a continuing encounter and sensitivity-training group, it would have to be goal directed. Even the smallest operating group, the family, has to have some sense of purpose. Amazingly, all human beings, if the educational system and the home environment from childhood onward were functioning properly, could be indoctrinated (a dangerous word?) that a full life, a self-actualized life, a life lived to its fullest potential, is a life of continuous, profound wonder over man, nature, and man's place in the ecological balance. This kind of wonder does not require the claptrap of theology. If enough doors are opened, enough questions are asked, both subjective and objective, a man or woman inevitably becomes a religious man or woman.

Beyond the question does Harrad exist (and the disappointment of hundreds who have written, even parents, eager for their children to apply) are the larger questions. What's so really different about Harrad than already exists in the premarital experience of the college generation? Are there in fact any actual experiments going on that point up the difference?

Numerous colleges and universities have combined male and female dormitories, but to my knowledge even those with wide-open parietal rules (Lambda Nu fraternity at Stanford, and several others, have admitted girls to the fraternity) have not created an environment where unmarried males and females live together. Where housing is available, the girls have their own rooms but haphazard interrelationships develop.

Rochdale College in Toronto, Canada, has gone a step

further. Here, condensed from *Newsweek*, November 25, 1968, is a description of their approach.

For Rochdale is unlike any college established or free—anywhere. It has no entrance requirements, no formal curriculum, no examinations, grants no degrees, and is not accredited by the Province of Ontario. Rather it is run and staffed and indeed owned by the students themselves—through the Campus Co-op Residence, Inc. which was formed in 1936 and now owns 22 residential houses in addition to the big new dormitory and has assets of more than $7,000,000. Initially Campus Co-op planned Rochdale as a residence hall for students attending the nearby University of Toronto, but last year a group that had been experimenting in communal living and free education turned the building into a showplace for their Utopian ideas about learning. . . . Rochdale residents range from 17 to 35; they are intentionally a mixed bag of radicals, revolutionaries, hippies and fairly straight people seriously interested in co-operative living. . . . The philosophical question of what is worth knowing is left up to the students themselves. . . . Rochdale takes a broadminded view of drugs and sex and is not concerned with the parietal niceties of most universities. Men and women live together in suites, and many unmarried couples live together.

Marshall McLuhan predicts that Rochdale has "all the makings of a Utopian flop." Yet it is interesting that in other writings McLuhan has predicted a return to tribal living.

From an Associated Press dispatch in 1968 by Curt Wolf, here is a similar experiment in the Free University environment.

Boys and girls are sharing dormitories at a student village in West Berlin—right down to the shower rooms. Schlachtensee Village was built in 1959 with Ford Foundation money and is run by officials of the Free University. Its dormitories house 450 males and 224 female students. . . . As a psychologist and advisor to the city government Helmut Kentler prescribed "total mixing." Kentler said: "Life in groups where the sexes are segregated is typical of repressive systems such as the army or police. It promotes aggressions, homosexuality and neuroses. But mixed living systems, on the other hand, are an excellent training for matrimony." Senator Werner Stein, member of the West Berlin city government for cultural affairs, commented: "As long as the new arrangement at Schlachtensee doesn't lead to disorder, I won't interfere. Indeed, if it works out better than the traditional plan, I might even recommend that it be adopted elsewhere."

While I cheer for the experiments going on in Canada and Berlin (and doubt if any university in the United States would dare to be so permissive, facing as they would the absolute certainty that state legislatures would call out the National Guard to prevent such improper use of state property), I do want to point out that these experiments, unlike the Harrad proposal, are unstructured and probably will founder, as do most attempts at communal living, largely because *they are not goal directed.* In essence they are simply broader manifestations of smaller unmarried groups and couples living together on practically every campus in the United States with the conviction that their sexual behavior is nobody's business but their own.

What happens to the campus "unmarrieds"? While any statistics in the area of premarital activity are open to question (even Vance Packard's personal survey described in his book *The Sexual Wilderness*), of the estimated five percent of college students who are living together unmarried I would guess that many of the couples are acting out a monogamous marriage. There is very little fluidity, and although there is no marriage commitment, the moral and the social commitment creates a situation analogous to monogamous marriage, with jealousy, possessiveness, exclusivity of sex, and trauma for one person or the other when separation (divorce) occurs. Thus while the campus "unmarrieds" do achieve some limited experience in interpersonal relationships (without the legal commitment), the basic difference from the going steady and the pinning or engagement of previous generations is that the sexual relationship is accepted without the former hang-ups.

While the campus unmarrieds are a step in the right direction, the Harrad environment, in contrast, would encourage (in a socially permissive context) the students to change roommates, experience several members of the opposite sex both interpersonally and sexually, while as a group, with someone to lean on (the Tenhausens or their

45

equivalent), they explore out the deeper meanings of sex as the ultimate form of both verbal and nonverbal communication between human beings.

I realize that a seemingly very narrow line separates Harrad and Proposition 31 from the advocates of swinging (multiple-partner exchanges) and free love. In the Spring Quarter, 1969, issue of *Ankh*, published by the Elysium Institute (see bibliography for address), Jefferson Poland, leader of the Sexual Freedom League which is active on several Western campuses including the University of California at Berkeley, asks the question "*What Is Sexual Freedom?*" and in a number of points defines it. Here are a few:

He/she enjoys sex relations intensely and often. I'm thinking of a tribe where everyone routinely expects to have five or six orgasms every night; if you have only one, your friends solicitously inquire about your health. He/she approaches the world orgiastically; will really BE THERE, open and accepting for every man, woman and child. He/she engages in sex and love affairs with persons of all races and creates an inter-racial family. He/she is a practicing bi-sexual, fucking freely with both sexes. He/she is immune to feelings of jealousy, and is capable of carrying on several relationships concurrently, as well as enjoying casual sexual encounters. However promiscuous, he/she also maintains stable and lasting emotional relationships with an intimate group of lovers probably living together as a "nest."

If any reader of *The Harrad Experiment, Proposition 31*, or *The Rebellion of Yale Marratt* believes this is what I'm advocating, they better read the books again! Poland's extremist position—multiple wife-swapping and the endless search for sexual gratification—is a blind alley. It is simply another manifestation of the campus religions of I Ching, Tarot, Witchery, Astrology, and a denial of man's potential, a negation and dropping out by ego-centered people hopelessly searching for easy solutions. Jefferson Poland doesn't shock me, nor does *Ankh*. In fact, I recommend you subscribe to *Ankh*. It's a quality printing job, the photography is excellent, and the males and females are beautiful people who happily show you their genitalia. These lovely people make love together and touch each other intimately. All very healthy.

Ultimately, *Ankh* may dare to depict copulation in detail. The Swedish magazines do—in living color! (See bibliography for one publisher's address.) And I think this a good idea, too, for the truth is that before we can ever discover how to express the subjective wonder of sex in photographs or the cinema, we probably have to pass through the childhood phase of shock for the sake of shock ... until the whole business becomes unspeakably boring.

And that's the danger of group sex. Despite the paperback cover of *Proposition 31*, which advertises that the author of *The Harrad Experiment* is now on a group sex kick, I am convinced that several men and women or dozens of men and women copulating together destroys the basic elements of beauty, depth, and communication, and loss of identity and ego which are possible in sexual intercourse between *two* people but which in group fucking simply become an athletic contest. Better to masturbate; at least in masturbation you can commune with yourself! Hence you will note that InSix in *The Harrad Experiment* and the Herndons and Sheas in *Proposition 31* have multiple sexual experiences but *as couples*. They function together as a group but make love *separately*. In their lasting relationships they are not whambang strangers but friends who enjoy each other, with all their foibles, as human beings.

It is fascinating to me that in the dichotomy that separates the free-love advocates from their opposites, the John Birchers (who at the moment are hell-bent on stopping sex education in the schools and pillory Mary Calderone and the Sex Information League), I am a reactionary in both camps. At the very time this Introduction was being written, for example, the Michigan state legislature passed an antismut bill with penalties up to ten thousand dollars for the sale of books or magazines depicting sadomasochistic abuse, flagellation, or torture, *as well as acts of sexual stimulation or gratification*.

The really sane way to approach censorship in a society of presumably normal human beings would be to censor any writing, photography, or communication that *devalues healthy human beings* vis-à-vis other human beings. Using this approach, not only would sadism, flagellation, and torture be censored but so would man fighting and killing other men. Think of the novels, movies, television shows, and Vietnams that would be eliminated under that formula! On the other hand, sexual stimulation between the male and female (even between homosexuals and lesbians, dead end though that may be) is by no definition a devaluation of the human being; we would have free nudity, and grow up quite accustomed to seeing joyous copulation in the arts and life. Under this definition, I believe the aesthetic kudos would go to the artists who portrayed sexual relations to the subjective limits of their media, and the devalued and ugly efforts would disappear along with stag movies.

The other day I passed a well-dressed elderly man carrying a placard in front of a local church. It read, "The Essential Mission of the Church Is People Loving People." If religious leaders—Catholic, Protestant, or Jewish—could convince me they really meant these words I would immediately return to the fold. Sadly, the vast majority of church people who would give lip service to this message are so entangled in the Christian-Judaistic moral teachings that many are doing their best to water down the sex-education courses given in high school. This, in spite of the fact that the sex courses in high school are at their best peripheral and do not dare to come to grips with the world the way it is. Instead of boldly tackling pornography and devalued sex as it is portrayed in every aspect of modern life, the high school teachers go blithely along teaching Charles Dickens, or George Eliot, or expurgated Shakespeare. We are in sad shape when the parents whose values are completely mixed up demand the right to perpetuate their sexual confusion on the next generation. Do they really want their sons and daughters to be so repressed that in later life they are candidates for the one-in-ten people today who are either in mental institutions or running to psychiatrists?

Of course, the real problem facing SIECUS and other groups advocating the teaching of sex in the high schools and grade schools is that in any given locality there are few people emotionally equipped to do the job. Even those who are available are afraid to stick their necks out for fear of finding themselves not only in conflict with parents but with other teachers who in their history, English, and social science courses should be correlating the present with the entire history of man as he has groped through the ages to comprehend his sexual needs and the frustrations imposed upon him by his fellow man.

The hundreds of sex manuals readily available in paperback (the only source of sex instruction that the average person receives) scarcely get to the root of the problem. Most people are still too shy to ask or discuss, so they can only read, and reading is a lonely act. In the October,

1968, issue of *Medical Aspects of Human Sexuality* (published only for the medical profession) an article titled, "Sex as Work" analyzes fifteen of these how-to-do-it books which are currently on sale and have a total distribution in the tens of millions of copies. The overwhelming conclusion of a study of the sexual techniques advocated in these manuals is that the height of joy is produced by *a combination of deliberation and management on the part of the male.* Sex as laughter, sex as pure joy, sex as an act of sheer wonder and defenselessness culminating in the miracle that one person can trust another to surrender fully, is still only vaguely comprehended in the puritanical work ethic of America.

Essentially, this work ethic and the endless pursuit of material pleasures and possessions in a culture based on money values have not only perverted our normal sexuality and our driving need for deeper intimacy and closer interpersonal relations but are at the root of the questioning and rebellion against the purposes and direction of Western culture.

Millions of children must grow up in the brick, cement, and steel urban environment and live and die rarely ever seeing black earth. Crowding them into ghettoes (white and black), we have created a nightmare world where man can never realize his human need to be a part of things growing, of the change of seasons, of the warm earth beneath his bare feet, can never know the joy of shedding his clothes and playing naked in clear, unpolluted water, or rolling naked in green grass or new-fallen snow, or digging in mud, squirming in it, or burrowing in fallen leaves, feeling the warmth of their decay against his flesh, or being at one with birds, squirrels, and even the lowly insects pursuing their own destinies in a plot of grass, or most important of all, know the sharing and the intimate contact of friends daring to reveal themselves to each other.

The hippies, by refusing to succeed, by refusing to perpetuate the system by any form of endeavor, may be lying down in front of a steamroller (sadly, they don't even care), but they have performed one invaluable service. They have forced us now, before it is too late, to ask the question: Where has the society gone wrong that hundreds of thousands of young people no longer can find a sense of purpose or values in the way we live? Here is a description of one overlooked aspect of hippie commune life, from a classic letter to the *Village Voice* by Vivian Gornick, May 29, 1969.

Children are everywhere definitely a part of the hippie scene. ... Children are handed around to all men and women like common property, so that there is an intimacy there between all children and all men and women even though every kid is ultimately accountable to his own mother. How do the kids respond? Almost all of the children I saw were beautiful and healthy and a good deal less hysterically selfish than they are where I come from. ... But the most important thing about the children is that they are a key to the most vital phenomenon of the commune, the re-creation, the redefinition, so to speak, of the family. I am deeply convinced a new, a *real* family is being formed. What I mean is this: there isn't a person in the Western World who doesn't bear the psychic scars of family life. You're supposed to love your father and your mother, and you don't. You're supposed to be close to your brothers and sisters, and you're not! And this terrible discrepancy rips you apart as long as you live. Here, I think the gaps begin to be closed, the wound begins to heal. People find they are close to those they're *supposed* to be close to ... i.e., those they are living with—because they feel spiritually akin. One feels, and in some places this spirit is alive with power, that here on the communes affection, and therefore concern, grows out of a bond deeper by far than automatic attachment. That bond is the acceptance that comes of intimate knowledge born in an atmosphere of stress and spiritual confusions shared. These people *know* each other in a true sense.

Not only is it interesting to contrast the hippie commune with the Israeli kibbutz (read *Children of the Dream* by Bruno Bettlcheim), but it is the potential of other ways of living (not for the hippies but for the vast middle class) that I have been exploring in *The Harrad Experiment* and *Proposition 31*, asking the question which my generation has ignored but which you and your children will have to answer. Is there a mid-position? Is it possible to create premarital and postmarital environments and, ultimately, stronger family groups and life styles which provide the individual with warmth and love and personal security from the group as a part of his basic necessities as a human being? Is it possible to create a culture where *living* and *being* are just as important as the individual's work contribution to the society (the sum total of individuals functioning together)?

We can never remove the impersonality and the achievements of a technological society, yet, I can't believe that man will be defeated by his machines. We got this way because this is inevitably where preceding generations, *unthinkingly*, led us. But *knowing* why and how, we can shake off the dead hand of the past. Let's not lose this age of protest. For those of you under thirty who will inherit the political machinery at a younger age than my generation did, my hope is that you will translate the protest into action to re-create not just a nation but the entire world. We need an autocratic democracy based on the manipulation of capital that works for all men. That means *leaders who dare* to get into the fray ... not dropouts and not perpetual graduate students in search of nirvana.

Basic to all this is caring enough about man and individual men and women.

To really like and enjoy people, not because they reflect your own ego, but simply because the short time that you *are* and they *are* is a mystery sufficient unto itself.

13

One of the delights in the many letters I have received is to hear from people who have recommended books I may have missed reading or who have told me about various experiments and new approaches to living. It may be surprising to many, for example, that I had not read Heinlein's *Stranger in a Strange Land* until a reader suggested it to me after *Harrad* was published. A reader in Michigan made me aware of Eleanor Hamilton and her writings ... and so it should be, a two-way feedback between author and reader. At the very least it gives a feeling that we are not alone.

The titles in the following list are mostly oriented around *The Harrad Experiment* and *Proposition 31* but do not appear in the bibliographies in those books. At the moment, for those who are curious, I am convinced that much of modern man's malaise is environmental and I am working on a novel which will involve a new type of communal living within the core-city area. Perhaps the protagonist will be an activist or a Norman Mailer type, who may never get elected mayor of New York but who with his monorail concept (and just because he is Mailer) should be. In any event, this has led me into reading widely on the cities and the urban prospect, and also to the amazing amount of creative writing by black writers. No undergraduate should accept his degree until he has read *The Autobiography of Malcolm X* and the writings of Eldridge Cleaver and Stokely Carmichael—which are only a beginning. From these hints, you can anticipate some political activism as a road to self-actualization!

The starred books are in paperback.

Bettleheim, Bruno. *Children of the Dream, Child Rearing Techniques in the Israeli Kibbutz*. The Macmillan Company, New York, 1969. Latency and adolescence in the Kibbutz compared with the same age span in American middle-class youth. Some fascinating conclusions.

Comfort, Alex. *The Nature of Human Nature*.* Avon Books, New York, 1968. Alex could teach a course in Human Values.

Eurich, Alvin C. *Campus 1980, The Shape of the Future in American Higher Education*. The Delacorte Press, New York, 1968.

Evans, Richard I. *B. F. Skinner, The Man and His Ideas*.* E. P. Dutton & Co., Inc., New York, 1968. A good introduction to the man who wrote *Walden Two*.

Friedenberg, Edgar Z. *Coming of Age in America*.* Vintage Books, New York, 1965. Here's high school, U.S.A. Scary!

Fromm, Erich. *The Revolution of Hope, Toward a Humanized Technology*.* Bantam Books, Inc., New York, 1968. If you haven't read this book, drop everything and do so!

————. *The Sane Society*.* Fawcett Books, Greenwich, Conn., 1966. Somehow, I forgot to include this book in previous bibliographies. It could change your value structure . . . for the better.

Gunther, Bernard. *Sense Relaxation Below the Mind*.* The Macmillan Company, New York, 1968. The Esalen Institute nonverbal communication techniques in easy-to-follow photographs.

Hamilton, Eleanor. *Sex Before Marriage*. Meredith Press, New York, 1969. If you are unmarried, with up-tight parents, make them read this book by a woman over fifty who knows the score!

Harkel, Robert. *The Picture Book of Sexual Love*. Cybertype Corporation, New York, 1969. Since this book will probably not be sold in most book stores, the address of the publisher is 80 Fifth Avenue, New York City. A sex manual. God knows there are too many of these, but this one with several hundred photographs is the first book or magazine I have seen that proves my belief that photographed sexual love can be beautiful and aesthetic in the hands of a sensitive photographer. This book should be studied by Hollywood moviemakers!

Harrington, Michael. *Toward a Democratic Left, A Radical Program for a New Majority.** Penguin Books, Baltimore, 1969. How we live sexually is a condition of how we live politically. With this in mind, this book and much of Harrington's writings relate to my own proposals.

Heinlein, Robert. *The Moon Is a Harsh Mistress.** Berkley Publishing Corporation, New York, 1968. In this novel and *The Puppet Master*, Heinlein introduces Line Marriage and Contractual Marriage. It's about time Heinlein wrote a non-science fiction book and developed his theories in detail!

Hilu, Virginia. *Sex Education and the Schools.* Harper & Row, Publishers, New York, 1967.

Kennan, George. *Democracy and the Student Left, Angry Students vs. the Establishment.** Bantam Books, Inc., New York, 1968. Students put George on the spot, but some of Kennan's views have merit.

Kenniston, Kenneth. *Young Radicals, Notes on Committed Youth.* Harcourt, Brace & World, Inc., New York, 1968. Interesting!

Laing, R. D. *The Politics of Experience.* Pantheon Books, Inc., New York, 1967. Not easy reading, but worth struggling through.

Lederer, William, and Jackson, Don D. *The Mirages of Marriage.* W. W. Norton & Company, Inc., New York, 1968. A different approach to interpersonal problems.

Leonard, George. *Education and Ecstasy.* The Delacorte Press, New York, 1968. Don't miss this exciting approach to the now-future of the joy of learning. As a senior editor at *Look* and vice-president of Esalen, Leonard proves that you *can* manipulate your environment.

May, Rollo. *Existential Psychology.* Random House, Inc., New York, 1960.

————. *Love and Will.* W. W. Norton & Company, New York, 1969. If you want to find in one place the entire philosophy-psychology that motivates me as a writer, it is in this book.

————. *Psychology and the Human Dilemma.* D. Van Nostrand Company, Inc., New York, 1967.

Otto, Herbert. *Guide to Developing the Human Potential.* Charles Scribner's Sons, New York, 1967. Sounds like a how-to-do-it book, but it is and isn't. Why doesn't some publisher issue it in paperback? Good reading to remind you of what you may have forgotten!

Perls, Fritz. *Gestalt Psychology.** Dell Books, New York, 1951. While I don't always see eye to eye with Perls, a member of the staff at Esalen Institute, he is worth reading.

Phelan, Nancy and Michael Volin. *Sex and Yoga.* Bantam Books, New York, 1968. In both *Harrad* and *Yale Marratt* I have suggested the joy of extended sexual intercourse. Since the Kinsey statistics indicate the average sexual act takes less than ten to fifteen minutes, it's obvious the experience is lacking a deep subjective interchange. This book doesn't have all the answers, but it will guide you into the act of love as an adventure in non-duality.

Rosenfeld, Albert. *Second Genesis*. Prentice-Hall, Inc., Englewood Cliffs, N.J., 1968. Contains some interesting thinking about the future of marriage and the family.

Roy, Rustum and Della. *Honest Sex, A Revolutionary Sex Ethic by and for Concerned Christians*.* The New American Library, Inc., New York, 1968. Excellent. Don't miss this book. Recommended reading for John Birchers.

Seton, Cynthia. *A Special and Curious Blessing*. W. W. Norton & Company, New York, 1968.

Slater, Philip E. *The Temporary Society*. Harper & Row, Publishers, New York, 1968. An excellent study of business and family life in a world of change.

Snitzer, Herb. *Living at Summerhill*. Collier Books, New York, 1968. Snitzer is in charge of the American Summerhill at Rye, New York.

Sohl, Jerry. *The Lemon Eaters*.* Dell Books, New York, 1967. A novel of a weekend encounter group. Well done and reasonably authentic.

Taylor, Gordon. *The Biological Times Bomb*.* The New American Library, Inc., 1968. This book will shake you out of your lethargy!

Watts, Alan. *The Wisdom of Insecurity*.* Vintage Books, New York, 1968.

Wilson, Colin E. *Introduction to the New Existentialism*. Houghton Mifflin Company, Boston, 1968. I had given up existentialism until I read this book.

————. *Sex and the Intelligent Teen Ager*.* Pyramid Publications, Inc., New York. Even if you are not a teen-ager, you'll find some of Wilson's ideas startling.

Odds and Ends . . . Magazines and Such

American Ethical Union. 2 West 64th Street, New York, New York 10023. A humanist organization worth considering. Dedicated to the belief that the highest value is human worth.

Ankh. Published by the Elysium Institute, Inc., 5436 Fernwood Avenue, Los Angeles, California 90027. Membership, which includes four issues, $16.00.

Change in Higher Education. A monthly, published by Science and University Affairs, 59 East 54th Street, New York, New York 10022. Sponsored by the Esso Foundation, proving that some of the Establishment is not afraid of an open forum.

Moscow News. Printed in English and airmailed weekly from Moscow. Annual subscription available at amazingly small cost from Four Continent Books, 156 Fifth Avenue, New

York, New York 10010. This newspaper won't make you a Communist, but it will sharpen your perception of the dismal lack of communication in the world.

Pace. A monthly with the format of *Life* or *Look*, but humanistically and youth oriented and upbeat (although *Look* has been more with-it lately). The December, 1968, issue of *Pace* is devoted to the subject *Are Families Necessary?* —with more to follow. Pace Publications, 835 South Flower Street, Los Angeles, California 90017.

Peking Review, China Pictorial (and others airmailed from Peking, China). Inexpensive and illuminating. Proves, at the very least, that we need Red China in the United Nations. China Periodicals, 2929 24th Street, San Francisco, California. Incidentally, there is no law against receiving these publications, and they may well make you feel that while we have a better ship, the captain and the crew often don't know how to make it run.

Playtime. Ostermalmsforlaget A.B. Box 5213 102.45, Stockholm, Sweden. This is the address of the Swedish magazine of the kind they haven't yet published in the United States. One or two copies of *Playtime* in full color will prove my thesis that once you have seen others make love (in detail) what is happening in their brains is more interesting than the connection of genitals!

Sex and the Contemporary American Scene. One issue of a quarterly journal published by the American Academy of Political Science, Prince and Lemon Streets, Philadelphia, Pennsylvania 17604. Your library should have it.

The Whole Earth Catalogue. Portola Institute, Inc., 1115 Merrill Street, Menlo Park, California 94025. If you don't find something you always wanted to know more about, or an idea to challenge your mind, in this catalogue, the originators will probably refund your money. $4.00 buys it.

The
HARRAD
LETTERS

The letters which appear in this book are a small fraction of the ten or more unsolicited letters I have received weekly since the publication of *The Harrad Experiment* in paperback. Unlike typical letters to an author, many of them were so revealing of the writer's personal life that permission to publish them was not solicited.

The following letters, which have been released by the individual writers for publication (whether they have permitted their names to be used or have preferred to remain anonymous), as well as the thousands that have not been published, have one thing in common. As "coming events cast their shadow before," all of those who have written me represent a fascinating groundswell—the beginnings of a tidal wave which I believe will usher in twenty-first-century men and women, and a world of deeper, more fulfilling interpersonal human values and relationships.

In encouraging The New American Library to publish this book, my hope is that by a continuing process of casting seeds on the wind, somewhere they will take root. It doesn't matter if the ultimate blossom is a Harrad College or a Proposition 31. What is important is for you to know that even in this age of seeming impersonality and individual loneliness there are a lot of "practical idealists" out there in the world seking answers and anxious to join hands with you!

BOB RIMMER
Quincy, Massachusetts 02169
September, 1969

June 15, 1968

Dear Mr. Rimmer,

As a student of sociology, psychology (social and abnormal), anthropology, folklore, economics, and political science, plus the science and art of communication, I found *The Harrad Experiment* and *The Rebellion of Yale Marratt* to contain not only a great deal of valid commentary on current people-problems, but also a number of *prima facie* sane ideas as to a few possible approaches to making this a better world for people. (I haven't yet determined if *The Zolotov Affair* was intended a part and parcel of this, or if it was for the "bread and butter" aspect of your existence solely).

In the estimation of myself (and of a number of other interested individuals in the Denver area), on the basis of a far greater than average knowledge (at the conscious level) of people's requirements for living (as above mere temporary survival) and of the mechanics of both the current "system" and the mechanics of social change, a number of your ideas are not only sane but also possible to implement in the current environment. Not only that, but the general atmosphere (socially and culturally) is such that I believe—on the basis of observable data—that it might not be too difficult to achieve a rather widespread acceptance and practice of such ideas in a comparatively short time *without* the turmoils that have in the past accompanied "mass movements."

If you would be interested in pursuing this further (or even if you wouldn't, for that matter), I would appreciate hearing from you.

If *any* of us are to survive individually; MAN (and other living things) must also survive. "People are for People." (Though *not* in the *usual* sense of being "for" something.)

Interestedly yours,
George E. Dew

P.S. Thanks for the opportunity your books have allowed for non-"down-trip" thinking! WHEE!

Dear Bob:

I was quite pleased that Challenge Press was so prompt in passing along my initial letter, and I found your answer quite interesting.

It was not too surprising to me that you do not make your living writing, as I am somewhat familiar with the pitfalls encountered by trying to have writing as a sole means of support. (My brother and I have both tried this, on occasion.)

Thank you very much for the information about Esalen and Kairos. I had already heard something of Esalen, but nothing really concrete, and I have been trying to find out where to acquire more information. Since receiving your letter, I have written both places.

I was not at all surprised at your statement that you are not an Ayn Rand type proselytizer. If you were, I doubt that you would have written the books as you did. (It is interesting to comtemplate where people are in relation to Miss Rand's concepts as compared to where they are in relation to yours.)

I am quite interested in obtaining a copy of *Proposition 31* as soon as may be.

I am not certain just which of my thoughts and experiences you would most appreciate (as I have only relatively lately come to appreciate many of them myself), so I'll "cast a seed on the wind," and we can go from there.

Approximately a year and a half ago I undertook an intensive study of communication. The end result to date has been (a) a permanent "high" without drugs or any other artificial aid, (b) a medically "impossible" improvement in various aspects of my physical condition, and (c) a complete reorientation (well, almost complete) in viewpoint toward people, happenings, and reality. (Erich Fromm would probably say that I have been learning how to be totally free; Scientology would say I am becoming "clear"; the hippies I know say I am "turned on"; most people don't know *what* to say.)

These results were obtained by approaching the problem of communication from the viewpoint that words are relatively unimportant, communication encompasses a far wider area than just the interplay between people, the basic purpose (or reason) for communicating is survival and the goal is to live, and a living being is far more than a mere collection of chemicals and electrical charges. (Please note, however, that I am an atheist.)

In terms of "group marriage," a number of years ago six of us had an interplay that was in fact *very* close to such an interplay; and to this day, notwithstanding the passage of time, there is a rather peculiar (in comparison to the usually observable) attachment remaining between at least four of the original group. (Spatial distance doesn't change this either.)

A year ago, a few of my friends were contemplating group marriage (after much study of *The Harrad Experiment*); and I provided the "moral sanction" they needed to implement action. The situation finally blew up when one of the members encountered a couple of internal hang-ups (socially imposed, incidentally) and refused to stand and face himself and work with the problems.

Right now, a relationship has developed between five other friends of mine (and two more are gradually becoming more involved) that, on the emotional and intellectual levels, has a great many manifestations of a true marriage. (In at least one area, there has been also a bit of the physical interplays—also—and this will probably spread as various remaining hang-ups are encountered and overcome.)

It appears to me that the very same hang-ups that lead to wars, to people dying between the time of birth and the age of 100, to most physical and emotional maladies, and to personal "selflessness" are also at the root of the troubles encountered in group marriage situations, in conventional marriages, and in all other potentially pro-Life activities.

Just as medical fact is that the human body *should* last at least 800 years (barring neglect or accident), knowledge of the nature of life-beings (and Man in particular) indicates that group marriage is a *far* more healthy (in *all* ways) state than conventional marriages, due to the exclusivity of the conventional marriage which destroys the individual's opportunities (in most cases) to grow in communication and understanding necessary for true happiness, productivity, and long life. (Superman is a Rat Fink!!!)

You might be interested that there are three small children (one just arrived) included in the currently developing relationship I described above. These children (the two oldest) have no fear whatever of people—strangers or otherwise. And no one in the "group" knowingly lies to or fails to accept communication of any kind from these children. Outsiders encountering these children for the first time usually find them to be a bit "strange" in relation to other children.

You might also be interested that any of us in the current group here can demonstrate that fear, anger, jealousy, guilt, anxiety, etc., are all *learned* emotions rather than being "natural," as asserted by a great many professional, religious, or philosophical teachings.

We can also demonstrate that ALL mental-emotional disorders are the result of some misunderstanding(s) and can be remedied without drugs, hypnosis, or surgery—*providing* that the person suffering from the disorder *really wants* to remedy the condition. (Allowing them to want such is another problem which, though more difficult to handle, we have also been able to approach with some success.) The key is contained in a knowledge of TOTAL communication, games conditions, and the true nature of life-being.

You might also find it interesting that, for me, the abilities I have described are the result of integrating knowledge from such divergent sources as the Bible, Buddhism, Erich Hoffer, Ayn Rand, psychology, physics, astrology, Erich Fromm, Plato, sociology, L. Ron Hubbard (Scientology), political science, economics, accounting, parapsychology (ESP), *yourself*, myself, games theory, folklore, astronomy, biology, Nietzsche, Spinoza, electronics, semantics, and communication.

Some of the integration and computation is strictly my own; and some of it was done by others, such as yourself (but checked by me for validity before acceptance).

In my estimation, the basic problem is not that other people—in general—don't know what I know; it is rather that they don't know what they know. The result of this not-knowing is internal conflict that leads to a computation of inadequacy, then to a computation of futility resulting in "opting out" via death (which only substitutes one set of problems for another for the life-being).

In contemplating relationships between people, I am reminded of "The Junkman," from Ken Nordine's L.P. *Son of Word Jazz*, wherein Ken says, "We need our need of NOT-needing each other," and, "Come, take hold of my hand! I am no braver than you, and you are no braver than me." When people come to *know* that they know this, it is interesting what happens to their shields and barriers against full trust and communication with others—friends or strangers.

I thank you!

George Dew
Denver, Colorado

4/11/1967

Dear Mr. Rimmer,

As I write this letter to you it is 3 A.M. in the morning and I am night-clerking at the motel whose address appears above. I have just finished reading your novel *The Harrad Experiment*. I enjoyed it; but this is not a fan letter. I don't think I've ever written a fan letter and if I ever should it would be to someone who needed one, not someone to whom it would be a nuisance. The reason I am writing to you is because I share many of the ideas and attitudes that you manifest in your novel, and I would like to do something about them.

First of all, I am operating on some assumptions that I have made about you, which may or may not be valid. I assume that you believe in the concepts that you have expressed in your novel. I aso assume that you may be interested in doing something to manifest these ideas. I further assume that you might be able to use me, in some capacity, in such an endeavor.

Now, if my first two assumptions are correct, I must somehow identify myself to you before my third assumption has any validity. Very well. I am ————. I am married and have one child. I am 29 years old. I have a B.A. in English from a state college. I taught high school English for a year and a half. I resigned because I couldn't teach garbage I didn't believe in.

I have taken a job as night clerk in this motel while seeking a job that I can believe in and give myself to wholeheartedly. I have been spending the late hours reading Yoga, Vedanta, Buddhist writings, and other philosophies that were sadly lacking in my formal education. God! I've learned more on my own in a month than I learned in four years of college!

I am convinced that I must find fulfillment in my life by serving my fellowman (extensions of myself and of God), loving him in some creative way.

While I was in the Navy (1957–1961), I came under the influence of Dr. and Mrs. Russell of Swananod University. If you know them and their philosophy, I need say no more; if you don't, further reference to them is not too important.

Writers like Aldous Huxley, Philip Wylie, Whitman, Sri Yogananda, B. F. Skinner, and Gibran have influenced my thinking.

I am a mystic. I believe in God. I believe in man. I believe in love. I believe they are all a part of each other, inseparable.

I seem to have an ability to communicate with people, to explain new ideas and concepts to them without frightening them.

Long before I read your novel I had a dream of a Utopian world in which all races had intermingled and the color of most people was a dusky roseate peach color. In this society people lived and loved freely. A man worked at what he loved to do. Everyone loved everybody else completely. In one vivid part of the dream two young people were unashamedly making love in an open cabana, designed for that purpose, along a beach in Puerto Rico and an old man with white hair came and watched them make love. His eyes filled with tears. He knew that they knew he was watching, and he knew that they loved him and he was somehow a part of their union.

I believe that life can be like this if man develops a new consciousness founded on love. I think it's worth working for.

I hope I have given you a fair indication of who I am. If you are actively involved in some project or work relating to this sort of thing, please contact me if I can be of service.

Writing a letter like this is strange. It is a form of baring oneself. I have a tendency to feel a bit embarrassed. You see I am extending myself to you naked and vulnerable—trusting in your love and concern, of which I have no personal knowledge. And this is poorly written.

Sincerely,

May 15, 1967

Dear Mr. Rimmer,

I'm very challenged by *The Harrad Experiment*. I also am at the beginning of preparing an "educational" series for the N.Y.C. listener-supported radio station WBAI. The series would explore the theme "High School Classroom Without Walls." It is my assumption that the size and nature of current architectural forms in schools seriously limit the imagination of educational planners. I want to assault these limits with a barrage of suggestions of significant educational experience that tend to be precluded by the existence of the classroom as a center of what is called education. Other considerations to be entertained are the legal aspects of "compulsory miseducation" and McLuhan's idea of the undeveloped country of the adolescent.

It occurred to me that in the context of your Harrad ideas you might be interested in this series of radio explorations, interviews, lectures, panel discussions. WBAI has extremely liberal programming, unlike any other stations except its sister stations on the West Coast. There would be no pay in it for you or me. To me the thorniest and most central question for high-schoolers is the one of sex and love that you raise in *The Harrad Experiment*. And we have among WBAI listeners parents and teenagers ready to entertain the Harrad ideas. It was a high school boy who gave me your book. How can the *many* potentially productive educational experiences be worthwhile as long as the question of sex and love is so widely skirted? Incidentally, I see arising from the sort of closeness that you provide for in *The Harrad Experiment* the sort of generalist that we are calling for today.

I hope that you will want to think further about a WBAI program regarding the implications of *The Harrad Experiment* for high schools. Sometimes I get to Boston but I'm hoping business brings you here.

Very sincerely,
John Wires
New York, New York

Dear Mr. Rimmer,

I was very pleased to read *The Rebellion of Yale Marratt*, having already read *The Harrad Experiment* and having seen you on the Allan Burke Show. I am myself a college student (a senior), and art major, and I feel that although still idealistic and somewhat unfeasible on a practical level (NOT because it *can't* work, but others won't *let* it work) your philosophy is beautiful and very sound! I imagine you have read *The Three Sirens*, which also deals with the idea of polygamous group relationships, however on a more primitive anthropological level.

I am one of the originators of a group called S.O.M.E., Society Organized for Mind Expansion at Rutgers University. (A publication called *The Modern Utopian*, Tufts University, P.O. Box 44, Boston, Mass. 02153 lists it and numerous other organizations that I KNOW you will be interested in. Please write for their magazine. It's a "digest of the major activities and progress of liberal social change agencies and intentional communities," etc. Please read it.)

My particular purpose in writing to you is twofold. First, to commend you on some fine ideas which mark you, in my mind at least, as a leader and "hero" in an age of anti-heroes (I don't mean idol, but rather a "hero" in the sense that you are brave enough to challenge the entire Judeo-Christian-American way of life . . . we're all human, though). My second purpose is to tell you about psychedelics and what the hippie generation's philosophy is, as I understand it . . . the reason being that it coincides with what you are trying to expound! Unfortunately, the image of the hippie as an immature rebel for rebellion's sake (as the newspapers have tried to show, with the exception perhaps of the Village newspapers and some periodicals) is totally inaccurate. It is exactly analogous to what happened in your book to Challenge, Inc., when the newspapers (compliments of Pat Marratt) get hold of an ad describing Challenge, Inc. The picture was not a pretty or accurate one . . . dig? Well, the vast majority of hippies and the "turned on generation" are nothing more than intelligent, educated, mostly middle class youths (predominantly) who are fed up with a country which is more concerned with killing (wars), materialism (money), and hatred than it is with the very essential needs for life: LOVE, BEAUTY, PEACE, HOPE, MUTUAL WORK to achieve goals, elimination of poverty, etc. (you know the rest . . .). Although psychedelics (such as marijuana (pot), L.S.D. and mescaline, and hashish) are only a *means* (which most hippies realize), they are quite effective in making those using them see through the futility of wars, hatred, and playing the game of acquiring money, power, and materialistic wealth. But, *MORE* important than this, they enable the users to experience a feeling of unity with his humanity and fellow human beings; of love and respect for his fellowman; of sexual attraction and beauty in expressing it, in a desire to "beautify" his world: philosophically, spiritually, artistically, musically, literarily, etc., and in a greater feeling of compassion for his fellowman. Your expression of God as being Man himself, "I am God," "You are God," "She is God," etc.,—is another "revelation" which is common to the psychedelic experience. Perhaps you feel that the use of psychedelics is harmful. This is *not* true and I would be glad to present you with documentary evidence (such as James H. Fox's (Ph.D.) report as Head of the Food and Drug Administration's Bureau of Drug Abuse that marijuana is not addictive, etc.) concerning psychedelics which you yourself could read and refer to. Perhaps you feel that chemicals are "unnatural" and "unnecessary." This is true and almost all hippies are aware of this. They realize that psychedelics are unnecessary and so they rarely use them, and when they do it is in a very *meaningful* way—in building and expanding a relationship, a FULLER and MEANINGFUL RELATIONSHIP, between two people. But, if this is your complaint, then movies, books, poetry, coffee, lollipops, and ice cream are unnatural and unnecessary. . . . At any rate, I and many other very intelligent and well-educated *productive* people believe psychedelics are a very important tool for spreading and living your philosophical viewpoint. As intelligent beings they realize that psychedelics are one of many *means* to reach the same *end*— your conclusions that man must learn to relate to many diverse individuals in meaningful, productive ways and must create a better world to live in, without hatred, wars, etc. Your "Mat Chilling's" philosophy and commandments are precisely what psychedelic revelations are all about—and you, and I, and others know we don't *need* pot or LSD to realize those conclusions, but it helps to reinforce them and make them much more logical. Finally, I suppose psychedelics are aphrodisiacs as well as euphoriants . . . the *orgasm* one experiences when high is inconceivable to the straight person who has never had his senses expanded and who has never prepared his nerve-sensory-endings for *full* stimulation.

I welcome you to try some form of psychedelics—but *don't* take my word about them. Read scientific analyses, both pro and con viewpoints, and speak to people who have tried them, and then, as an individual, *decide* for yourself . . . and please let me know what your decision is. I believe that you (and your wife—wive(s), no doubt) must be beautiful people and I hope that you too will enjoy the sensory and spiritual experiences psychedelics have to offer. The sensory experiences with LSD or mescaline (visual, auditory, tactile) have no equal or comparison to ordinary sensory experiences and have a beauty which exceeds the power of words to describe them.

If you would like a bibliography of references, or have any questions, I would be more than pleased to help and answer you. In any event, I hope to hear from you. . . . Are you going to write more books, form a community, etc.? In hope that we may all learn from one another and grow within-without—PEACE, LOVE, HOPE, FLOWERS, BEAUTY, MUSIC

Serena Friedman
Newark, New Jersey

P.S. In my own media of ART I hope to make my contribution. . . .

14 August 1967

Dear Mr. Rimmer:

It seemed I no more than finished speaking with you than the whole world caved in to the point that I've just now got around to writing—nothing of any consequence, but I've just now come up for air.

My opinion of *The Harrad Experiment* remains as it was—perhaps it would be more accurate to say my opinion of your theory—although there are parts I cannot go along with. I wonder if I would ever be able to knowingly share a man whom I loved with other women—or if he could. I wonder where all the flirting and other—umm—goodies would go under a system such as this. I find the manipulation of the public (as expressed in the InSix term paper) somewhat horrifying—although I should imagine this is primarily due to an absolute refusal on my part to open my eyes and see for myself to what extent I am manipulated now. Punctuation can go hang—also typographical errors—I'm doing this with one eye on the Highway and expecting my boss any moment and I have a slight horror of being caught with a personal letter in the machine, and on company paper, too!

What a relief to read your book—particularly that section from approximately page 150 to 200. I dearly love this part of Arkansas to live in but the possibilities of getting the caliber books you mention in your addendum are rather slight—it is quite easy to obtain Havelock Ellis (but when you are forty who needs him?) and others of the same ilk, but, Good Lord, it took me three months to acquire a copy of *Sex and the Office*, and I got leered at then! It has always seemed odd to me that people (particularly women) could look at unsanctioned sex as putrid, kicks, bigger than both of us, and always as leading to apple pie and vine covered cottages—but never as fun. People seemingly have no conception of love as such—perhaps it's mainly early conditioning.

I'm making little sense and rambling badly—my mind is a mélange of thoughts and questions. I have been happily single for some time now—again happily, with many opportunities for whatever sex life it took to keep me contented—so it quickly became apparent I wasn't after a roll in the hay—per se. It seems to take your whole body, plenty of time, a lack of impatience, sweetness, thoughtfulness, and a great deal of humor to come up with a totally satisfying experience—there are few capable of achieving such (in my experience) and so I am necessarily speaking from small experience.

I was quite amused at your evaluation of *The Three Sirens*—I first read the book some time before my divorce and at the end of a seven-year "drought" and I practically foamed at the mouth just thinking of such, although the idea of taking just whatever happened to be on duty at the Community Hut left me with a feeling of "Oh, Hell, you can't win them all." I cannot say much more without revealing more than I should—suffice it to say my thoughts were abruptly and delightfully changed to "Oh, the poor things! Such a shallow way of going at it."

Some of the statements you made over the phone help tremendously—and in other ways these statements only frustrate. To know there are others like me is very comforting—by the same token, infuriating. How and where and when—I guess I'm more lonesome than anything else.

I'm looking forward to receiving your earlier book— perhaps by the time I have digested that one my thinking will have solidified a little.

Thank you again for the book I've already read—I'll get back to you after reading the other.

Sincerely,

P.S. I don't really flit all over the country via telephone— only when a given idea especially strikes me—as did the Dogpatch, U.S.A. ideal. I'm not really a nut—I just look, act, and think like one.

July 15, 1967

Dear Mr. Rimmer,

I have just finished reading *The Rebellion of Yale Marratt*. It affected me exactly the same way as *The Harrad Experiment* did after I had finished reading it. I have never read two books that gave me as much satisfaction as these two have. The message in both of them is one which I believe in deeply. I feel that you have the answer to the quest for peace and love among men. The utopias that you write about are neither farfetched nor impossible. The sooner that man learns the true beauty of love between people and the intensity that it may reach, the sooner he may be at peace with the world. I am just a college student, yet I can recognize the overwhelming feeling of love that your characters in these two books profess. I believe that love can become so magnificent and great as to engulf individuals and make them feel as one. I feel that you have found the perfect way to put your ideas and hopes across in these two books. The bigamy laws of this country are archaic and outdated. They reflect a past buried in the religious belief that sex and love were dirty and sinful and ought to be covered up. It is certainly possible for a man to love more than one woman at the same time and to love her so much as to feel that they are one. I encourage you to keep writing on this idea of yours and to keep telling people that love is not a single feeling. After reading these two books, I find it very difficult to keep trudging through one weary day after another of our "modern" world. Thank you for two wonderful books. I support your ideas all the way. It is too bad that neither InSix nor Challenge, Inc. exists, because they would have a place.

Sincerely yours,

11 June 1967

Dear Mr. Rimmer,

Mat says "... the inability to communicate is at the root of all misunderstanding." And in trying to define love, he says, "... foremost that I find it very easy to communicate with you both in the surface of words and the deeper understanding that lies unspoken between us."

Well, you have a magnificent ability to communicate, and something very beautiful to say. And I love you for having said it.

The challenge of *The Harrad Experiment*, or just the "Challenge, Inc." is not a wild, crazy, impractical dream. Truth, whether or not it can immediately be utilized, is its own justification. Surely the truth about the nature of social man is as exciting and practical as learning the surface temperature of Betelgeuse.

No, what is really impractical in the long run is the premature cynicism, the sophomoric attempt to appear worldly-wise, which prompts the, "Aw, you can't change the way people ARE."

This cuts twice: the tacit assumption of the intrinsic

evil of man, and denial of the possibility of historic social progress, of new ways in education, even of curing human sickness—that is, an argument at once antihumanistic and anti-intellectual. Once I told my wife that writing a poem, or even sharing another's poem which is well-loved, is like an act of love: one is completely exposed. It takes a particular courage to leave oneself "naked to laughter" as Shelley put it. Your writing is so wide open, I want to rush in and say, "I know, I understand, I love you."—and I suppose that leaves me equally naked to laughter. But how can one touch unless he opens up, and where are we if we cannot reach out and touch?

Incidentally, I find another value here. You mention "Dover Beach" in a certain lovely context—the first time Yale and Anne sleep together—and it is so appropriate here—a little flood of warmth wells up in me. This is very far removed from the pseudointellectual game of name-dropping. Rather, it is a kind of symbol which stands for an important feeling, such that when you use this, I know instantly a great deal more about Yale Marratt—and presumably about you.

(I will toss one back at you which you will either know, or will look up—Stephen Spender's "I Think Continually of Those Who Were Truly Great"—and this again, not to try to impress you, but because this poem states so well why I think you are truly great.)

There are about a million questions I want to ask you. Have you read a novel by Robert Heinlein (science-fiction) *Stranger in a Strange Land*? It is not a great literary work (in particular I found the female characterizations weak), but it has strong elements of *The Rebellion of Yale Marratt* and hence is a fine book, and I also love Heinlein for having written it. There is a similarity in the religious sense of love as a cohesive force, etc.

Next question. You know, for a 42-year-old man, I am still terrifically naive. When I read *The Harrad Experiment*, I was convinced that it happened (was happening?). I did not view it as fiction, but fact. And I am still uncertain. I still have the feeling that this is real, but for some reason (because of its—shocking—nature??) presented as a novel.

The most important question I will defer until I've told you something of myself. I am a physician, graduated in 1965, now in a dermatology residency in Chicago.

It is a measure of the temper of our times that I don't expect this admission to elicit any particularly favorable impression. Not that I am ashamed of my profession, but rather that it does not now evoke an image of erudition and humanism that it once did. Further, the age of forty seems rather advanced to obtain a medical degree (even if I did obtain a couple of degrees before it), so that I am unable to claim brilliance—merely a kind of dogged determination.

Anyway, the question. The most important question. What can I do to help? This would be easier if you imagine an invisible coupon from an invisible book, *Spoken in My Manner*, mailed back to you with (admittedly) an invisible $10!

No wait. I am willing to concede that you are a brilliant writer: that you have brilliant ideas and set them down on paper. That there is no Harrad University, no Carnsworth Foundation, no Challenge, Inc.

What I am not willing to concede is that these were merely entertainments. Your ideas are too deep, too profoundly moving, too concerned with a humanistic salvation of man. And would you not build Jerusalem "among these dark Satanic mills"?

So. I am not a wealthy man; I'm probably not even very bright. I don't believe in an organized religion; I'm sure I don't even believe in God according to most definitions. I'm not a crusader, belong to no organizations, have no influence. Yet to the depths of my being I understand what you are saying, and am committed to it. It is in this sense that I ask—What can I do to help?

Sincerely,

24 June 1967

Dear Bob,

Thank you so very much for your kind and thoughtful answer to my letter. And let me preface this one by saying that I am *not* trying to engage you in a sustained correspondence; I don't wish to intrude on what must obviously be very precious time. In fact, I am amazed at what must be tremendous powers of organization to carry on a full time job and still write so well. And it's a sort of terrifying responsibility to try even to acknowledge "hundreds of letters"—especially when they come from well-meaning and friendly people.

Now I have tried to think how to phrase what I want to say next without it sounding stupid or frivolous—I can only say it in a perfectly straightforward way: I consider you my friend. Like in the fable of the lion and the mouse, I do not see at this point how I ever might be of service to you (whereas you have already benefited me greatly), but I can only tell you my intentions are clear and pure. If you should ever need me, if I could ever be of the slightest service, I hope you will remember what I have written here.

To borrow a phrase from a very fine writer and a beautiful person whom I know: I admire you wholeheartedly.

Warmest regards,

November 4, 1967

Dear Mr. Rimmer,

I have just finished reading *The Rebellion of Yale Marratt*, and I would first of all like to thank you for writing such a beautiful book. If only more people would think as you do, then maybe the goals of Challenge could be realized. But unfortunately, our "Christian" society cannot even accept the preachings of Christ, which are very similar to those of Challenge, so how can we expect it to go one further and recognize that all men are God, and for that reason we should love them.

I have one question for you in relation to your book. You say there are ten commandments of Challenge. However, I have read the third section of your book four times, and I cannot find the fourth commandment. Is it included? If so, could you please tell me what it is.

Once again, thank you.

Sincerely,
Adrienne Rosenberg
Buffalo, New York

May 25, 1967

Dear Bob:

Again, let me repeat my appreciation for the "as if" exercise called *The Harrad Experiment*. I have turned the book over to Humphrey Osmond but he has not as yet read it. I look forward to his reactions.

The same night I spoke with you on the phone I called up the outfit down in Freeland, Maryland, and yesterday received their literature in the mail.

My impression is that their premises are organic gardening, an agrarian anarchy, opposition to vaccination. Sadly, another variant of withdrawal from efforts to change society. Some weekend, however, I'll drive on down and visit them.

While in my third year of psychiatric residency I had the opportunity to visit another effort of communalism, one of the operations of the Church of the Golden Rule at Willets, California. This is a commercially successful ranch that is run soundly by an experienced administrator with a committee of elders handling the theologic considerations. The theologic group apparently has little practical decision-making functions.

Their system is total. Although marriages are conventional, the children are cared for in a communal nursery and educated in the ranch school. The school is accredited by the state, the teachers, picked from the young women of the ranch, are sent away to a nearby state teachers college and housed in a mobile home owned by the church.

When a person joins the church he donates all of his possessions and, in turn, is cared for by the group. The member is given ten to twenty dollars per month for clothes and pocket money.

The church has several similar operations such as hotels in Los Angeles and a greenhouse operation in Southern California.

They maintain an impeccable business relationship with

the community and operate on a cash and carry basis, a new operation being adequately funded.

The effects on members seemed to be less than optimum for features of vitality and striving. A fellow physician who had quit general practice in that area to come for psychiatric training at Mendocino State Hospital had served the ranch, population fifty to sixty, and noted them to be rather tender in the face of stresses of childbirth, serious illness. He found them dependent and child-like.

Another difficulty they are having is the attrition of the young adults who prefer the *Sturm und Drang* of the outside world instead of the bland, isolated agrarian life with the characteristic repressive attitudes of conservative small town Christianity.

I would enjoy revisiting this brave utopia that appears to be somehow headed eventually for some sort of disintegration because of certain customs. Because their premises of the nature of the individual seem to be limited to the conventional Protestant theologic concepts they have little chance of bending to the temporal, visceral needs of the members.

Perhaps there is a need for internal stress in a group to challenge and demand the individual show his excellence by rising to the occasion and by rebellion against or constructive achievement.

Appreciate greatly *Yale Marrat*. Thank you. Will read it when I get time in my busy bureaucratic life.

Warmest regards,

Tod. H. Mikuriya, M.D.
Acting Director
Drug Addiction
Treatment Center
San Francisco, California

March 9, 1967

Dear Mr. Rimmer:

I have just read your book *The Harrad Experiment* the second time and my enthusiasm keeps increasing! This is one area where much work must be done. And your manner of putting these issues before the public is much like the "scout" of old frontier and Indian days. I am very interested to see how the book continues to be accepted. I, for one, find the field fascinating and am always looking for new sources of material.

This experiment you describe is one I would be interested in finding out more about, but I have run into a small snag. The Dr.s you mention, the Tenhausens, are perhaps pseudonyms as is the Journal and the college and I am sure this was done to protect the experiment, but I was wondering if a copy of the article that Dr. "Tenhausen" wrote in 1959 or 1960, with or without the real names, could be obtained? I realize, if I read correctly, that this experiment may still be going on; so a continued respect for the real information would be honored.

I realize I am a stranger out-of-the-blue asking you to do me a favor, but if I may I'll ask only one more. You include in your book a partial list of readings for the Human Values course; would it be possible to obtain a more complete list? I would be grateful for any help and would be interested in hearing from you and Dr. "Tenhausen" about the progress of this experiment.

Will your book have a follow up? Yes?

Until I hear from you, I remain

Respectfully,
Walt J. Cotton
Topeka, Kansas

7 March 1968

Dear Mr. Rimmer:

I have just completed *The Harrad Experiment* for the second time. I will undoubtedly read it again in the near future.

The design of the experiment, the concept, basically is sound. Or so it seems to me. I could easily identify with various characters in the book, and enjoyed not only the expression of a new social idea (at least new to the present social order), but also the bubbling humor that punctuated the serious thoughts.

I do wish such a social grouping could exist, but fear that, generally, man is not ready to accept love on that basis.

Speaking personally, I can say only that I'm amazed at my own capability to accept what love I have been fortunate enough to find.

I am married, no children, and after sixteen years I realize that there probably won't be any. But my energies are expended in other directions. As an example I have thirty-seven bids in our area, all wondering when I will come home from Vietnam (next June—I'm sure!).

I would normally read a book such as yours, and enjoy it, then forget it. But in reading *The Experiment*, I got the distinct impression it could be a possibility.

If this theme was simply the mechanization of your mind, it was well done. If, however, it indicates your belief that the universal love and acceptance of man is possible, then count me among your advocates.

I do believe that such a group can, and in fact in many cases, does exist. Perhaps not on the scale pictured in the book. But I also know, of a certainty, such a group would be destroyed by the present society.

Though I am far from well-to-do, and certainly unable to entertain on a lavish scale, I would like to offer you the hospitality of my home should you find youself in the El Paso, Texas, area.

This, for ulterior motives of course; I would like to discuss basic ideas such as are in *The Experiment*.

I'm rather a conforming nonconformist in that my nonconformity is mental rather than exterior. But mentally capable of thought.

After June, '68, if you are in the area, please feel welcome to accept my hospitality and call.

I would like to hear from you regarding your motives in writing *The Experiment*. Who knows, perhaps one day your ideas *may* change the world.

Sincerely yours,
Jim Dodson
El Paso, Texas

Dear Bob:

I received your answer to my letter the other day, and would have answered sooner, but the demands of a war leave little time for the pleasant things in life, such as writing letters.

I will look forward to meeting you one day, and showing you our hospitality, but let me warn you beforehand. After ten minutes in my home, no one is considered a guest any longer. I'll get you the first drink, coffee, or otherwise, after that—you fend for yourself. It then becomes your home, too, for as long as you're there.

My wife and I both prefer that people not just "make themselves at home," but that they truly feel it is home. So if you do make it to Texas—be welcome—we would enjoy your being there.

By way of a friend in Poughkeepsie, New York, I've received a recommendation on *The Rebellion of Yale Marratt*. —She said she was going to read it again to see what she could "learn." She was, at one time, an extremely jealous woman. Not so now.

Anyway, thanks for the answer, and I wanted to restate the invitation to visit.

Right now, I have to go to war, so take care of the country back there for me.

Hope to see you in Texas.

Jim Dodson

January 28, 1968

Dear Mr. Rimmer:

This is a difficult letter for us to write, never before having written to an author.

We have read *That Girl from Boston*, *The Harrad Experiment*, and *The Rebellion of Yale Marratt*, which we believe to be your latest novel.

Your writing has left us feeling interested, curious, and very stimulated.

We realize that your time is valuable, but hope that you will be able to spare a little time for us.

Would you believe that we want to know just about everything you can tell us about yourself?

We are interested to know, in obtaining information for your novels, how you are able to express so many private and personal feelings of a woman, which we feel a woman would not even tell another woman.

We would like to know of any other material you have written, how we may obtain it, and if you are presently working on another novel.

Being avid readers, belonging to several book clubs, we are eagerly awaiting your next novel.

We would be most happy to receive a reply from you in the very near future.

Very sincerely,

Dear Mr. Rimmer,

I wish I could adequately express to you just how much I appreciated your consenting to talk with me, and just how much I enjoyed our conversation. You are a most stimulating thinker and convey very effectively the excitement you seem to find in your thoughts. I only wish that all my sandwich lunches could be so fascinating.

Thank you also for your generosity, for the lunch and especially the Perennial Philosopher Christmas Cards. You certainly know how to make one feel welcome and at ease.

I do hope we can get together again sometime next semester. Best of luck in your book now in progress, and may you and your family have a very joyous and meaningful Christmas season.

Thanks again,

Sincerely yours,
Robert Pettit
Cambridge, Massachusetts

Dear Mr. Rimmer:

I am about two-thirds through your book *The Harrad Experiment*, and find it one of the most stimulating books I have read in several years. I find its handling of sex and values in American society path-breaking and thought-provoking.

For me, the book has a similar mood and theme to Herman Hesse's *Sidhartha*, in which the main character has a quest throughout the book to find meaning in life and what values he should live by. In your book, I enjoy the close interweaving of fiction and reality so that sometimes they are indistinguishable: in this respect, your book is reminiscent of Eugene Burdick's novels *The 480: A Novel of Politics* and *Fail-Safe*, both of which I enjoyed immensely.

I am writing to you because of my curiosity about the fiction-reality continuum in your novel. For example, the maturity and insight shown by the couples who compose the "InSix" seem to be far beyond their chronological years. I wonder to what extent this maturity and insight are a product of the Harrad environment or a product of your maturity and insight. A coworker in my office, who received a master's degree in Anthropology from Columbia before becoming a city planner, commented that in fictional accounts based on actual journals, there is always the problem, Where does reality end and fiction begin?

In view of this, I would very much be interested in reading studies which may have been done by social scientists on the Harrad College experiment. My undergraduate background in sociology stimulates me to view the Harrad experiment in human interaction as a natural for study by sociologists or other social science professionals. If any studies have been done, I would appreciate knowing by whom and where they are reported. Also, is Harrad College (or whatever it is called) still functioning? I assume, of course, that the novel is based on an actual experimental college and is not entirely fiction, which it may be.

My own particular interest at present is applied sociology, specifically in the urban field. I will begin work for a Masters in City and Regional Planning at U.C., Berkeley, this fall. I did my undergraduate thesis on the topic "Interaction and Friendship Formation in Suburbia: Is Diversity Desirable and Possible?" I was trying to answer the broad question, "Does the balanced community approach and philosophy have a valid application for today?" For example, what happens when a community has residents of varying socioeconomic background, race, or religion living in close proximity? Is the result unbridgeable conflict and daily friction, or can there be a meeting-of minds or sharing of different values or tolerance of different points of view and ways of doing things between people of varying backgrounds? I have tried to explore these questions through library research.

At present, I see the new town or planned community as a potential vehicle to mix people of varying backgrounds in a kind of melting pot which center cities never achieved because of sharp segregation within the cities and because people fled them as soon as they had the income to live in suburbia. New suburban tract housing is often of a narrow income range, which means a homogenous makeup of residents in terms of education, occupation, or other socioeconomic elements. It is possible that the new towns of Columbia, Maryland, or Reston, Virginia, will turn out to be more of a melting pot than our large cities have been. Since there is no data available to support this contention, it is blind optimism on my part that this will happen, based on the values and expectations voiced by the developers.

Besides hearing about any studies which may have been done on Harrad College, I would be interested in the kind of work you do when you are not writing novels.

Sincerely,

Dear Mr. Rimmer,

Never before have I written a letter of commentary to an author, least of all in protest. I am not a very pushy (assertive, aggressive) person, but your book has provoked me.

First, let me say that from what little knowledge and (alas) experience I have, the sexual-freedom aspects of your book are great. If I hadn't thought so much of it from that angle in the first place, I would not have bothered. I read infinitely worse things than yours—even on the points where we disagree, but I consider you an ally, so I want to pick bones.

My disagreement comes not on sexual or "moral" matters, but rather on educational ones. While your book was very very exciting and stimulating (directly as well as intellectually) for its sexual aspects, I found the educational philosophy rather unfortunate. I hesitate to say old-fashioned, because I have no greater respect for many of the new-fashioned ideas than for the old.

My first big bone to pick was your apparent assumption that psychological tests are any good. Having taken several courses in this subject, I have slowly come to the conclusion that despite (because of?) my own rather spectacular showing on some of them (it got me my present job, my position in graduate school!) they are quite primitive. First of all, there are many assumptions which test-makers make that go against your philosophy and mine. It is difficult to discern this, but I am becoming more and more convinced that their way of testing people is superficial and primitive.

Next, the notion that people should be tested at all. I was very favorably struck by your notion of competition against the unknown rather than against each other. My only real bone to pick here is the apparent premise you have that intelligence is relatively fixed. This is the common notion—the idea upon which intelligence tests were invented, etc. Recent extensive research in intelligence, using the tests which were invented to discern how much of a certain immutable stuff called intellectual ability is around, have shown that it is quite fluid and can be greatly improved. I am *not* by any means talking merely about diadvantaged. I also realize that I have already put down educational tests en masse, and that includes intelligence tests; but I believe that what the test-takers have finally learned from their tests is what I felt before I knew of their results: that intelligence is a bit more environmental than genetic.

So, it would seem that your principle of dividing up the people in your Utopian school according to ability would be a very disastrous way of (1) focusing attention on one criterion variable or set of variables, and (2) giving up far too early on those who would not pass.

I agree that many people have been forced into an academic mold who did not belong there. I think that the academic mold should change, however, and that another premise you seem to have—that covering actual subject-matter ground is important in itself—is false. Learning to think is not the result of studying any particular subject matter. Obviously, any progress made in the ability to think must be done with raw materials such as exist in the books you mentioned—but I think that the educational environment existing around Boston is sicker than the sexual one—and that's pretty damned sick!

I am presently a victim of the sexual sickness, but not so much of the educational one. I take courses which are usually quite atypical. It can be done and is being done—at a state university. Many, I'll wager. First of all, there is no grading, in effect, at my own particular level. Grades are given, but most faculty members do not like the idea; all B's is a general rule. If you do no work or don't show up or something, you may get a C or D. If you make a scene, or need an A, you may get it. Otherwise, grades are usually completely deemphasized. Having been in this program for three and a half years now, I assure you that in no other way than by this method could this department have completely changed my life-philosophy, or at least made me aware of my own.

I found your apparently unexamined Protestant-ethic, work-is-holy orientation a shade disappointing in the light of so many of your beautifully expressed ideas. You riled the hell out of me, in fact, by writing what I have long wanted to write—a story of healthy people! I am so goddamn tired of reading about the tail end of the human spectrum. Your book was a definite relief.

Don't confuse my philosophy with many that are going

around. Don't pigeonhole and forget me. I have pigeon-holed you above, but mostly to make a point—and I have not forgotten you.

Let me speculate a bit. I sincerely believe that work is on the way out. I work forty hours a week, and go to school twelve hours a week. Despite the relative absence of grades, my schoolwork is very taxing, not because so much is required, but because it is interesting enough that I work at it on my own. My job is also very free. Mostly I just read what interests me and contribute my opinions to a three-man staff which writes documents on educational policy. My real passion in life is music—modern music. I write, listen, and read about modern music far more than I should for my own good. I could very very easily turn out to be a composer, but not unless I can get enough money somehow to forget working forever.

Because of the time of day it was offered, I landed last semester in a course in job counseling. It was there that the philosophy of the value of work was given to us, rather dogmatically (not in my department). I then realized that I do not value myself by what I produce, but by what I am. I produce when I need to for myself, not in order to value myself as a producer.

On the other hand, I value humanity and feel I can do something to help. I want to make it better purely for selfish reasons. I enjoy people and I want to make them more enjoyable—this is not superficial, just frank. It is probably the real motivation of your book, too; along with a desire to be remembered forever, which you obviously have, and which I share.

I have your bibliography. I shall read on it conscientiously until or unless I get bored and/or disappointed. I suggest you reread *Summerhill* and *Freedom, Not License*, as well as some of Maslow's and Rogers' latest.

I hope it will not insult you if I say I thought your book was crudely written here and there, and that I liked that very much. The crudities were not intentional, and were probably crudities to few besides me, but I felt that you were a bit too conventional in your utopianisms again and again.

But obviously I don't believe in the remove-the-beam-from-your-own-eye philosophy, because I think that saying "maybe I've got a beam in my eye, but at least that makes me some kind of expert," rather than keeping your mouth shut. The secret is never to give plank-eyed advice without making an honest and real (none of this "well maybe I shouldn't say anything, but . . ." business) admission that

83

you are kind of hung-up and stupid but maybe your own sensitivity and projection make you a valuable psychological lookout, etc.

I will close by saying that Harrad sounds like Goddard to me. I admit that I heard about Goddard from a very enthusiastic person, but it sounds as if you went there, or that Bates is another Goddard, or something. There are no Tenhausens at Goddard, I gather, but several of the qualities are present; the problems people have in screwing more than one person, the realization that you don't have to screw who you don't love, the eventual feeling of love which spreads, etc. I kept recalling my friend's often quite similar comments. Maybe you're both indulging in a prevailing daydream?

I do hope you will write to me. I am very much interested in what you are apparently trying to do. Even if you are merely trying to make money (I don't really mean "merely") I still admire you greatly. If I have bitten at a lure at which you are inclined to laugh, forgive me; I am not offended, but I think you do give a bit of a shit for the world. If there were more of what you write about around, the world would be a hell of a lot better to be in, and I think you want your world to be better for you, at least (if not at most).

What kind of business do you run, anyway? or is all that a bit of invention? I hope not. Dishonesty is kind of lazy and sad.

S. Whealton

Dear Mr. Rimmer,

Thank you for writing. I am flattered that you, being busy and distracted, etc., took time to dictate a letter. I hope I don't shock your sensibilities too much when I confess that I thought your letter was an ad. I nearly threw it out unread except that I never do that with anything. If it had not been for the word "Sherbourne," I might never have divined who you were, for I never read the name on an advertisement.

Since writing you, I have thought a great deal about what you have written. I have also lately become very much interested in cinema. Is there any plan for a movie of *Harrad*? If so, I urge you to try to pick a decent director, etc. I am quite tired of good books and bad movies.

A friend of mine who owns a bookstore thinks your

book is inaccurate. To him, your idea of loving more than one person is great, but human nature is inexorably tied up in the old system. Your book represents to him a false hope. My own feeling is that he is wrong, and is perhaps justifying his own ability to come only so close to your ideal by believing that he is doing as well as is humanly possible. He actually believes that any such experiments as you suggest either fail and revert to the old system or turn out to be an introduction into complete promiscuity and an inability to attach emotional bonds and meaning to another person. He sounds like an ad for the old system.

I wonder how to change things. I suspect that economic considerations will do the job for us at their own pace; when people are no longer usable economically, their puritanisms will have to fade. There will be exotic stoicisms and current mores will die with a long bang, not a whimper; but time is compressed; centuries of subjective time pass now in a decade, and the distant future I see is distant only in terms of events, not of time.

I thank you again for your letter. Strangely, it was dated July 24, 1967. Usually I do not notice such things, but the letter was scrutinized in every detail. It is strange what silly contingencies guide thinking.

Please do write. I thank you for your attention.

Cordially yours,
Stephen A. Whealton

Dear Mr. Rimmer,

I have just finished reading your book entitled *The Harrad Experiment*, published by Bantam Books, copyright 1966. The book was by far an experience in itself.

The book was written in such a way that it tended to lead the reader to believe that the pilot study at Harrad College actually took place. My feelings, as well as those of many of my friends, regarding the experiment are that the book is in fact the truth, not just a figment of the imagination.

I do not feel that our society today would accept such a

vast turn of social and moral conduct if it were made public knowledge, although our social and moral standards have changed tremendously through the years. I do feel that many years from now your theory might be accepted.

For educational purposes and to satisfy my own mind, I am interested if this experiment actually transpired, and if so, were the results within your realm of expectation, and if so, do you plan to continue to pursue this form of education? If not, I would like to know why or what caused you to be inspired along these most controversial lines.

I would like to say that your book has caused much discussion among our group of friends, both pro and con. But we have all agreed that it was well written so as not to lose interest in any part of it. This in itself is talent!

Very truly yours,
(Mrs.) Charles E. Van Dyke

Feb. 10, 1968

Dear Mr. Rimmer,

Just this week I read *The Harrad Experiment* with great interest and enjoyment. For some time I've contemplated the idea of a new kind of communal living and your novel helped a lot in stirring my imagination to new depths.

A group of friends in —— are discussing the possibility of geodesic domes for small communities. What the problems would be are not clear to me now, but we're in the talking stage at least.

I'm wondering whether you're reading *Psychology Today?* It would seem to me that people who've actually *experienced* the living you fantasized would have some new thoughts, too. I'm thinking of those who've experienced Kairos or Esalen in California.

Carl Rogers has been quoted as saying (Dec., 1967, *Psychology Today*) that more "pictures" are needed of what changes a person goes through when he has had an experience with an encounter group. He feels that the best answers will come from *living* people who can express their feelings.

Have you considered doing follow-up work on such people? I'd love to hear.

My best,

Dear Mr. Rimmer,

Your letter arrived today and I'm answering immediately because my mind is flooded with ideas as a result of your suggestions.

I'll be awaiting the arrival of your novel *The Rebellion of Yale Marratt* with great enthusiasm. Discussing ideas is one of my great delights in life and I'll write again after reading the novel. Thank you for all your warm suggestions and kindnesses.

I feel more alone than I should, perhaps, despite your reassurances that I am *not* alone. Many people here in —— respond to my ideas, but when leadership is needed I seem to be a pioneer in need of a sharp knife to cut through the jungle of inhibitions. I'm a widow, age forty-four. I think young. I feel young. Most of my friends or associates are under thirty.

I could write a book on my life and philosophy, but perhaps it would bore you. Martin Buber, Norman Brown, Abraham Maslow, and others have influenced me very much. On a personal level, my deeply intimate relationship with a very loving Negro man has probably been the greatest stabilizing force in my life. (I'm white.) I'll be glad to elaborate with you if you wish, but, for now, I'll just limit my remarks to these.

Ask what you wish. Human truth is my passion.

The plans our group is making are very simple for now. We want to have a form of communal-living experiment on a farm this summer. We are in great need of suggestions. I'll look into the ideas you've expressed. (Magazines, etc.)

I'm hoping to attend Kairos this spring in order to become more emotionally prepared for leadership.

I'm interested in parapsychology and also believe that our earth is probably being observed by other civilizations. I am *deeply* concerned about the survival of the human race.

"May Man Prevail?" Erich Fromm asks, and so do I. I hope "he," or "we," *shall* prevail. *No* thoughts are too radical for me now.

Warmest regards,

Dear Mr. Rimmer,

I had the happy accident of buying *The Harrad Experiment* for weekend reading two days ago; I was persuaded by the cover art that this would be a casual and entertaining comment on our contemporary society and its foibles. But what I found was potent enough to engross me from the dedication to comment about your search for a fulcrum.

First, I would like to state that offering my opinion to people I don't know personally is no pastime of mine. In fact, the last time I did so was in the form of a diatribe to a magazine of the *True Confessions* ilk at the tender age of thirteen, telling the editor what a literary dunghill the entire publication was. Oddly enough, instead of dismissing me as a crank, they sent me a ten dollar check, neatly pigeonholing me into their Opinion Poll file. However, the warm glow of Harrad has compelled me to write this letter, but I'm afraid that my thoughts may not be too organized due to my enthusiasm.

I am not saying that I agree with you 100 percent in a flower-child optimistic fashion; there are several minor points that from my own well of experience and knowledge I feel may or may not be effective socially. But I am glad to find another person in this insane society who is in mental harmony with me. There seems to be something on almost every page that is deserving of volumes and volumes of discussion and writing, and hopefully very large active efforts in reality.

Thank you so much for the bibliography; before I discovered it, I was ready to compile my own via red pencil and list. I see we have been influenced by several of the same authors, and I could offer comment on a few more.

I would like to know more about your plans for setting your ideas in motion. Is the InSix thesis of infiltrating a city and state government your plan or only an idea? And is there now, or are there plans for a Harrad campus? A

Holiday magazine article I read last summer on Antioch College seems to come close to Harrad. And the campuses of Berkeley and San Francisco State continue to feed the local newspapers with juicy and unorthodox little tidbits of gossip about the living arrangements and uncensored nature of the classroom materials and discussions. But Harrad would go a lot further than either of these, with their blessing and sanction.

As a college student, I have been tempted to occupy the comfortable niche of one who has formed his own philosophy of what an ideal society should be like, and go on living the life of conformity, condemning all those who didn't also adjust, as if philosophy could only be a mental exercise. This could only make a hopeless cynic of me (and hypocrite), which I refuse to become. I *am* optimistic about man's nature; all he needs is the education and enlightenment to avoid all the pitfalls of ignorance and psychological hang-ups that ruin him. My approach to other people has been of the golden rule variety ever since I can remember, and this evokes such awe in most people that they miss their chance to take advantage of my vulnerability.

I'm a junior undergraduate now, and I plan to go to medical school and be a doctor (perhaps a pediatrician).

I don't know what I could offer you if you are indeed serious about taking an active role in evolving society, but perhaps you would be interested in my observations of people my age group on campus, or perhaps in the engineering field, where I am working now (I get involved in discussions whenever time and workload allows, on any subjects that come up). I would be more than glad to answer any inquiries you may wish to ask, if you feel my perspective may be of help to your ultimate goals.

Sincerely,

December 1, 1967

Dear Mr. Rimmer,

During my reading of *The Harrad Experiment* and *Yale Marratt*, the question came up as must with many of your readers, "Do these ideas work in practice or only in a novel?"

Of course, I may be taking you much too seriously—like the country bumpkin who rushes up on the stage to rescue the heroine from the villain. But, just in case the point of view in these books does happen to be your own, I should very much like to know what happens when you expose actual people to this amount of freedom. It obviously depends on the people, so perhaps the heart of my question is "Have you tried?" and if so, "What happened?"

To be perfectly frank, I have more than a passing interest in what you may have uncovered. Not that I go along with those who hold that enough freedom solves everything—the hippie world is not my idea of heaven—but every so often a small group of people do succeed in combining a high degree of interpersonal freedom with reasonably responsible behavior while still preserving that spontaneity and rapport that leads one to wonder afterward, "Why can't it be like this more often?"

Which perhaps boils down to, "are you the right person to talk to—or do I keep on looking?"

Again, thanks for listening.

Sincerely,

Dear Sir:

This is just a follow-up to our telephone conversation in regard to *The Harrad Experiment*. As I stated, I am twenty-one years old—twenty-two on May 7th, and am an avid reader, preferably something with body, a mind-expander as such, not just wishy-washy sexy books. Your book is one of the few books I have ever really gotten excited about. What really shocks me is the fact that there exists a non-puritanical, outward thinking, mind in Quincy, Massachusetts.

I've just recently returned from California, being a resident there for the last six and one half years. I ran away from here at age fourteen, probably the wisest thing I ever did. My family, as such, consists of my mother, a resident of W. Quincy, my sister, an R.N. at Q.C.H., and grandparents (millionaires at that), who reside in Hingham. Since you are accustomed to New England psychology, something I never could and probably never will understand, you realize why I am considered the family blacksheep and unwelcome everywhere but my sister's home. This is neither here nor there; what I can't comprehend is why you haven't been tarred and feathered or burned at the stake, or is it that people here couldn't absorb what you tried to present?—and most excellently, I might add. I wish that there were other words that I might use to explain how your book captured the very essence it sought. I would, except that my conversational English is adequate, but my spelling and penmanship are atrocious. You have just added one more fan to your list of readers. I will now endeavor to obtain *Yale Marratt* and *Proposition 31*, as well as any others I can get my hands on.

This is the first time I've ever written an author of a book that I have read. I have met Mrs. E. Gibbs, author of *Gunfodder* and others; she writes beautiful thoughts, with no relation to actuality. (My opinion only), and I met the drug addict Ken-something-or-other, who wrote "The Cuckoo something-or-other"; both (Ken and book) left me unimpressed.

May I say here and now I have gained something from your book that has enlightened my senses, and my admiration for your talent as a writer and creative thinker is very close to envy. I wish that I could set to words the thoughts I've had on certain phases of my life.

Although I'm (as they say) *only* twenty one, I've worked at many and varied jobs, from a grain mill, to a copper mine, and finally ending up as a Marine Master Plumber, achieving most of these jobs by lying about my age. I have spent some time in a reform school at age twelve and thirteen; my mother didn't feel it necessary to have a boy around, since my father had left her. For that I can't blame him; he couldn't have done a better thing for himself. Please excuse lack of motherly love, I find it impossible to comprehend, which no doubt, adds to my independent thinking and bad manners. I have been around the world once and a half if you can call it that. So, although a boy in the eyes of most, I rebel silently, with reading and without the use of a beard. The truth being I can't grow one of the damn things; I shave every six weeks whether I need to or not.

My God! do I ramble. My only complaint on the book

is it was too short, but I'll get *Proposition 31* as soon as possible. Please, Mr. Rimmer, keep writing; it gives the nobodies of the world, myself included, the ones who have discovered your talent, a sort of one-upmanship against the so-called establishment.

Thanks again for the use of your mind.

Yours truly,
Michael A. Kemp
Rochester, New York

January 17, 1968

Dear Mr. Rimmer:

Having read and reread *The Harrad Experiment* I find myself wanting to communicate directly with you. Your ideas seem to be exactly the answer to the contradictions of our changing ethics. Certainly what passes for WASP morality today is not any answer to basic human needs— if it were, the hypocrisy surrounding man-woman relationships would not exist. The hippie's idea of love is a revolt, which results in free sex, but not in the freedom of deeply understanding another human being. The Harrad approach is so "senseful," so human, that I find myself testing all social experiences by Harrad standards. What is of major concern now is to transform ideas into action. What can be done to further the ideas outlined in your book? Here are some proposals.

The Harrad College idea is neat but would require convincing quite a few parents of the wisdom of a whole new morality. Better to concentrate on talking with young people themselves. The cities would be logical starting points, since within a small area are enough people receptive to the Harrad idea. How to find them?

Why not a Human Values course to be given at night?— not necessarily even a part of regular college or university? This would attract not only college students but post-college students who are seeking an alternative to the suburban marriage-go-round. Through class participation and after-class discussions, a group of from twelve to twenty couples could be formed, much like the Harrad College living arrangements. The question here is if this would be enough people to match roommates successfully? One problem with too large a group would be finding living quarters large enough for everyone to live together.

Group members would either attend classes in the city colleges, or work during the day and take part in the Human Values seminar at night—probably a special class in their own house. Meals, housekeeping, etc., could either be done communally or by outside help (as in a college). After a while, smaller groups would no doubt form (as InSix) and these groups could then find a home and function more as a family. Needless to say, the whole plan would depend upon the right leadership, and a high degree of maturity on the part of the group members. If there were enough leaders, this program could be simultaneously carried out in all the large cities.

Of particular interest to me is the establishment of group living units (like InSix). The "two alone against the world" marriage sounds romantic but most often simply does not offer enough variety or stimulation for a thirty- or forty-year span. Boredom results in the couple having children to give the wife something to do, something to talk about when husband comes home. Either this, or extramarital adventures and/or divorce. Group living would infinitely expand the possibilities of being alive in all joyous aspects. It would not suit everyone but the option has to be available for those who do wish to live in this manner.

I have lived for the past two years in a communal group known as the Taliesen Fellowship. Started by Frank Lloyd Wright in 1932, it is still a thriving entity. There are about seventy people in the Fellowship—thirty-five staff members who are architects (Taliesen Associated Architects) and thirty-five students (apprentices). Members of the Fellowship live together both here in Arizona (October-June) and Wisconsin (July-September), sharing the responsibilities of cooking, building, maintenance, and clean-up.

After experiencing communal life, I can see the loneliness and frustration inherent in two people trying to be a whole group to each other. The answer lies in the creation of Harrad communities with the total living and loving commitment to each person in the group. I would like to hear your comments on these proposals for a grass-roots Harrad, and any other levers you are employing.

Sincerely yours,
Donald G. Kalec
Scottsdale, Arizona

August 8, 1967

Dear Mr. Rimmer,

I wish to congratulate you on your novel, *The Harrad Experiment*. Speaking as a member of the in-between generation (3/23/38), I think that your work has been one of the most important single stimuli that I have encountered in my life and I feel sure that it will exert an important influence on the remaining course of it.

I am a physicist (married and with one child) currently teaching at a small liberal arts college. Unfortunately, I can not speak for my own university when I say that if there is not now a Harrad College, then there certainly ought to be one. I do not believe the idea is impractical, and feel that the basic philosophy is a sound one. I may attribute my meager successes thus far in research primarily to an active intuitive sense. The ideas, reactions, and emotions that emerge from your characters strike me as being very real and correct. Intuitively, I feel that the Harrad idea represents a possible solution to the problem of man truly socially interacting with his fellowman. Surely if we proceed on our present course we are heading for disaster both on a personal and worldwide scale.

Since the dawn of time, man has feared what he could not understand. And in turn, he cannot understand what he does not know. In our present society it is virtually impossible to know one's fellowman, and thus to understand him. I do not believe that we will ever be able to live in harmony with one another until somehow we strive to break down this barrier. Thank you for the bibliography. Perhaps if each of us tries to educate our own family (without, I hope, social chaos), we may achieve some small measure of success. Surely it is time to attempt something! I think that perhaps this country is finally beginning to realize that something must be done. I am afraid however that any solution forthcoming will only be of a superficial nature.

Perhaps if enough of us begin to care we may be able to accomplish something. Keep up the good work.

Sincerely,

May 24, 1967

Dear Mr. Rimmer,

I spoke with you earlier this evening on the validity of *The Harrad Experiment*. I've just given it to a friend and she can't put it down either.

Your wedding ceremony was beyond description—what can I say? To quote you, "Abi gezunt."

I would be very interested in learning the origin of Harrad. In my life, I could never hope to propagate such an idea. I just can't believe it. Maybe it's my young impressionable mind (20½) at work, but I haven't read such a fantastic story in quite a while. This could be based on the fact that I'm presently teaching third grade in —— and my reading is mostly in *Finding New Neighbors* and assorted primers.

While my present plans for the future include graduate school (Columbia School of Journalism), I know I too will succumb to the mundane, urbanized idea of marriage and children. After reading *Harrad*, I'm ready to give back the diamond, cancel the caterer, refrigerate the flowers, etc., ad nauseum. But I won't, I'm sure. My background just won't allow it. God forbid I should postpone the wedding; I think it's a "sin" in Judaism. Don't bother to suggest that I forget my heritage. After ten years of Hebrew school, a bas mitsvah, living Jewish bobis and zaydes, and Conservative (leaning toward Orthodox) family, Friday night candles and chale, it would be a little difficult to start over again. I've decided (intelligently) for Judaism as my faith and I can't change now (don't want to change now).

Getting back to the reason for this letter. I would really enjoy discussing the book with its author or hearing more from you about it. I'm sure a fantastic mind such as yours would lend itself to a discussion that in itself could be called an experience. However, as I am through June 2 and you are diligently at work, there is little or no time. *But* I do live in Boston and I'll be here *all* summer. My husband-to-be (I think) will be returning to Boston this summer, and after making him read the book I'm sure he would be as excited as I am right now over the remote possibility of hearing from you or meeting and talking to you.

If you were serious about sending me a copy of your new book, I accept.

If you've survived this letter so far, let me add my thanks for writing a great book.

Sincerely,

January 27, 1968

Dear Mr. Rimmer,

It would, of course, be no surprise for you to be told that *The Harrad Experiment* has generated considerable excitement within the college community. It may be of greater interest, however, to learn of instances in which teachers have successfully employed the book as the literary presentations of a case for an alternative to present "accepted" attitudes toward sex and marriage.

I am taking the liberty, therefore, of enclosing a memorandum (written largely to disarm possible criticism) and a questionnaire with the tabulated responses of a class of fifteen freshmen. I shall be meeting with a much larger group some time in the near future. In this connection, there are a couple of points about which I am not entirely clear, and would much appreciate further comment from you.

1. While I take it that part of the argument set forth in *Harrad* is that a genuinely open and deep relationship to another person will, almost inevitably, be accompanied by sexual relations, a number of us were distressed at the weekly rotation scheme adopted by InSix following the birth of their first children. It seems to me, at least, that you attempt to draw a somewhat sharp distinction between "sex and love" and "sex for procreation" (though Jack at one point seems not to observe it). Thus, for example, both Sheila and Beth decide that even within InSix they wish to have their children by particular spouses. While I would grant that occasional and *ad hoc* relations are likely to occur given the living conditions, it does not seem to me that the possibility of such an

egalitarianism either could, or should remain a "live option" after the arrival of children. For surely at this point a new dimension to the act of intercourse has been added, a superadded concept which might be expressed as the thought, "This is the person whom I not only love, but with whom, and only with whom, I have created the most amazing love of all." I am arguing, in other words, that the arrival of children itself adds a particularizing emotional dimension to the sex act itself. The alternatives seem simply (a) an insensitivity to the implications of parenthood which is out of keeping with the otherwise perceptive nature of the individuals involved, or (b) a renunciation of the decision to have children by only one spouse—a true "group" marriage—of which we have no indication.

2. A second point about which I found myself disturbed concerns the somewhat excessive exclusiveness of InSix. It is not simply a question of difficulties in establishing relations with the "outside world," but even with Harrad itself. As sophomores, juniors, and seniors one hears no reference at all to anyone who has subsequently entered the school, and indeed, very little of anyone else in even their own class. Does the "depth" of their own interrelations preclude others entirely? I can understand the difficulties of really relating to the "uninitiate," and the manipulative aspects of the proposed "takeover" of the "State of 'X,'" but I am at a loss to understand the justification for ignoring even the other Harrad students. Love, as you never tire of saying, is essentially a giving and not a receiving ("It is better to give than to receive?"—rather liturgical, that!), but the group is far more "possessive" in its "love" than most monogamous marriages ever are. Such, at least, is my impression.

3. In sum, you place before the reader two distinct patterns. The first, or "normal" one, quite properly (in my view) accentuates the excessive frustration, guilt, repression, *et al.*, engendered by the standard course of events leading to marriage. The fraternity party, the sexologists' sequence of looking, touching, finally mutual masturbation, etc., leading to the "possessive" marriage "contract," ultimate boredom, etc., are all "stock" features, and it is easy to excuse the literary license involved in adding such rhetorical details as the hellish vistas of suburbia beckoning, women's clubs, *Time*, and chocolates. The alternative, of course, is Harrad College, with its open attitudes, genuine personal relationships, appealingly

bright students, and general vanguard-of-the-future atmosphere. Very good. But just where does that leave the existing college student of today? Yours is a "message" novel, but what part of its message is applicable to real students, students who must love—and ache—within at least the first stages of the nightmare courting procedures you have so accurately described? In the outside world, says Harry, a rapid shifting of sexual partners would be devaluing; not so within Harrad. My students have to cash their chips for more than utopian coin. Neither to be nor make another a sex object is only a small down payment.

4. You will, I hope, permit a final expression of uneasiness which has, at its core, a vested-interest pique. The next time you see Phil, suggest that the "thousands of ideas" approach to the construction of a philosophy of life is only half the picture. Human values are not alone the product of literature and psychology. He might consider Kant, Spinoza, Plato, Moore, and spend a week—no less—upon a single book, Toulmin's *Place of Reason in Ethics*. A little time with us "logic choppers" might disclose the truth behind a literal falsehood. It is not the case that jealousy is a man-made emotion, for it is seen in sibling rivalry and even dogs. But if we are to survive, it must be man-eliminable, which is what I think he really meant to say.

I hope you will not interpret the remarks I have made above as hostile, for they are not so intended. I should not have gone out on a limb and dealt with *Harrad* in the first place did I not think it offered more than titillation or emetic. *The Harrad Experiment* is a terribly relevant (in both senses) book for today's college students. You have seen the problems clearly, and something, I think, of the answers. I look forward to hearing more of them from you.

Sincerely yours,
Craig Stark
Painesville, Ohio

[Mr. Stark's memorandum and completed questionnaire follow.]

*Memorandum: To Members of Mr. Stark's G.S.
100 Preceptorial*

Despite a number of misgivings, I have decided to devote the next meeting of this Preceptorial to a discussion of Robert Rimmer's *The Harrad Experiment*.

This is a novel which many would classify as "sophisticated pornography," and most, perhaps, of those who would defend its "redeeming social significance" would nonetheless consider its viewpoint fundamentally immoral. It is a persuasive—and at times suggestive—apology for so-called "free love." It is thus precisely the sort of work whose consideration in a classroom could be turned into a *cause célèbre* by outraged parents, and it is my hope that this memorandum may avert any such embarrassment to the College. If my judgment that this work is worth our consideration is in error, the mistake does not lie in an irresponsible haste or lack of forethought, but in a misevaluation of the possible educational assets and liabilities.

My chief concern, however, is not with possible Administration reprisals (which in some institutions might range from dismissal to more subtle salary and/or promotional pressures), for LEC has a commendable tradition of respecting the considered decisions of its Faculty. Rather, my worry arises from a consideration of my responsibilities as a teacher to you as freshmen students. Frankly, the reading of this book will possibly offend some students violently, and might erotically arouse others. Either of these extreme reactions would not only cause personal pain, but would seriously jeopardize the possibility of your mature and rational consideration and evaluation of the book. In view of these possibilities, however, I wish to establish certain "ground rules" which will govern the next meeting of the Preceptorial:

1. The book is not to be considered "assigned" or "required" reading. As college students you must use your own good sense in deciding whether or not to read it.
2. It is expected, however, that those who elect to attend the next meeting of this Preceptorial will read the work in question *in its entirety*. Only on this basis can it be intelligently discussed.
3. Attendance at the next meeting of this Preceptorial is optional. A student who elects not to attend will not be considered "weak" or "prudish," for there are many reasons why you might decide that reading *The Harrad Experiment* is not the best use of your time.
4. We shall not be concerned in our discussion with determining literary merit, legal standing, or author's "real" motives. Rather, we shall consider the book as

presenting a serious proposal to alter our normal social attitudes toward sexual relations before and within marriage to conform more closely (as the author sees it) to more ultimate human values. Our discussion must be serious and honest, but must not force participants to disclose their own private actions. Our discussion, in other words, is to be an example of that kind of rational argument concerning values for which I tried to make a case in my Winter Vespers address. (Anyone who wishes to read that address in preparation may obtain a copy from Mr. Miller's office in College Hall.)

Subject to the provisions and qualifications I have made above, I do consider *The Harrad Experiment* worth consideration in a Preceptorial meeting. I have not only based this decision on the fact that several of you have asked that we take it up, though that in itself is one legitimate consideration. The novel seems to be "making the rounds" on campus, and, more fundamentally, the ideas it sets forth form an important part of the "Environment" to which you must relate your "Self." If personal values are to be determined on a more rational basis than either whim or taboo, they must be based on a consideration of arguable alternatives to present standards. *The Harrad Experiment*, whatever its "real" *raison d'être*, can be read in this light, and, on this basis I look forward to our discussion next week.

Craig L. Stark

DIRECTIONS: This questionnaire is an attempt to evaluate the experiment of considering *The Harrad Experiment* in class. It is completely anonymous and no attempt will be made to deduce the identities of the respondents. Feel free to make additional comments on the back. Do *not* sign your name!

The tabulated responses of a class of fifteen freshmen are indicated in the parentheses.

PART I. *The Harrad Experiment* as a presentation of an alternate system of values.

1. Would you like to be a student at Harrad College?
   (4) Yes   (4) No   (7) Undecided

2. Would you admire someone who could seriously consider it?
   (14) Yes   (0) No   (1) Undecided

3. Do you know college students who would like to enroll there?
   (1) A good many   (10) A few   (3) None

4. From your present perspective, do you think that the attitudes toward sex relations before and/or within marriage advocated in *Harrad* constitute a "live option" either for your generation or the generation you will raise?
   (7) Yes   (5) No   (3) Undecided

5. Do you believe the present patterns in undergraduate education impose *excessive* levels of sexual frustration on college students?
   (8) Yes   (5) No   (1) Undecided

6. According to your own best estimate, approximately what proportion of today's college students will have engaged in sex relations before they marry?
   (2) Over 75%   (9) 50-75%   (3) 25-50%
   (0) Under 25%

7. Do you believe that the description of male-female relationships among college students portrayed in the "fraternity party" episode is essentially an accurate account?
   (13) Yes   (0) No   (2) Undecided

8. Do you think that an InSix-style marriage would be preferable to the more normal American pattern in terms of ultimate human values as you conceive them?
   (2) Yes   (9) No   (3) Undecided

9. Assuming the 20-year "takeover" program for the "State of 'X'" were successful, do you believe that the life of a citizen living there would be richer and more meaningful than it would be in contemporary American society?
   (8) Yes   (2) No   (5) Undecided

10. Has reading and discussing *Harrad* assisted you toward clarifying and understanding your own personal values?
    (13) Yes   (1) No   (0) Undecided

PART II.   *The Harrad Experiment* as a work of contemporary literature.

1. As a contemporary novel, how would you rate the book?
   (0) Superior   (14) Good   (1) Mediocre   (0) Poor

2. Did you find the characterization and plot plausible and well drawn?
   (8) Yes   (0) No   (7) Moderately

3. Did you find it easy to identify with the characters in the story?
   (6) Yes   (1) No   (8) Moderately

4. Do you believe that the author's descriptions of sexual acts and his vocabulary were artistically justified in terms of the overall point of the book?
   (10) Yes   (3) No   (2) Undecided

5. Do you think that you have learned something about the nature of literary presentation of a point of view as a result of reading and discussing *Harrad*?
   (11) Yes   (1) No   (3) Undecided

PART III.   *The Harrad Experiment* as an aspect of the G.S. 100 program.

1. Do you think that reading and discussing this book within the context of the G.S. 100 program was justified in terms of assisting you better to relate your self and your environment?
   (15) Yes   (0) No   (0) Undecided

2. Do you believe that the "ground rules" were adequate and adequately enforced to make consideration of *Harrad* justified within the context of the G.S. 100 preceptorial group?
   (14) Yes   (0) No   (0) Undecided   (1) I didn't remember them.

3. Did reading *Harrad* impose what you consider to be an undue emotional stress on you?
   (0) Yes   (15) No   (0) Undecided

4. Do you think experiments such as consideration of *Harrad* should be
   (14) Encouraged   (0) Eliminated   (1) No comment

May 13, 1967

Dear Mr. Rimmer:

I have just finished reading your novel *The Harrad Experiment* and am so impressed with the new light thrown upon the values and morals of the younger generation that I am taking this opportunity to write you concerning this. I feel that if there ever was an experiment such as this I would like to be a part of it, not just for the sexual connections but more for the psychological and mental attitude which I believe becomes a part of the Harrad student. I take my hat off to you. The book was excellent. Before I close I would just like to convey to you that for some reason I am having difficulty locating the books *That Girl from Boston* and *The Rebellion of Yale Marratt*. I am very interested in reading them now.

In conclusion I hope this letter will be considered an inspiration for your future novels.

Yours very truly,
Robert Sugar

October, 1967

Dear Mr. Rimmer,

Your book *The Harrad Experiment* is indeed germinal— and in the twentieth century! It was referred to me by my brother; and I, in turn, referred it to several friends, who are, no doubt, referring it to others—and on and on. No words of mine nor those borrowed from a "great" can accurately express the intensity of gratitude and love I feel for you for sharing your philosophy with us—only my life and the lives I affect will do that. You have helped me to draw out of my mind ideas and feelings which before I could only probe unconsciously. And I love you for this—indeed, my capacity to love is growing each moment of life, which causes great enthusiasm and zeal within me. To my amazement, I also love myself more, and I'm realizing with this that I am now and will be even more "tomorrow" a beautiful person who is and will help this world by loving, and teaching love to my unborn children.

I am all smiles to know that I am on the right path to self-knowledge—a major key to love. Your book served as a catalyst for this—both the contents of the novel and the bibliography. Thank you so much for including the bibliography, because it, too, gave me a direction from which to begin. My life is evolving and will continue to evolve until my death, with a new enthusiasm and hunger for knowledge, work, and love. Before I read your book the first time, I feared at twenty-two years I had experienced all new things to life except pregnancy, but now I know that every day is a new life while met with a creative mind and open feelings.

Along with Sheila, Stanley, Beth, and Harry, I matured —not only mentally and emotionally, but as an artist (I am a student-painter). There is *so much* to see and study in such a familiar object as a shoe which has been worn for two years—it takes only creative, searching, and open eyes.

Thank you, Robert Rimmer, thank you for helping me to see, live, and feel more creatively.

> More than before,
> Judith Tomoff

December 20, 1967

Dear Bob Rimmer,

My silence has been too long, and so I now am making known my intention which has been with me since I received your letter and copy of *Yale Marratt*. I am still searching for those elements which make up Judith Tomoff. And still even harder is the search for that expression of myself through my paintings. When I feel that I have come closer to that, I would like you to accept a painting of mine, in gratitude for you sharing yourself with me.

Your letter and book could not have reached me at a better time—when I came home after watching Alan, whom I love with my life, fly away to Oakland in uniform (he is a medic in "Nam", now), I was frightened, lonely, and angry. I grabbed onto your extended friendliness and warmth, which *really* helped me. My first reading of *Yale* was for an escape—and escape I did! All I could do those first days was read and live someone else's life. I guess I couldn't stand the pain of my own. But time has helped in toning down the intensity of feelings and depression.

My feelings and thoughts about *Yale* are comparable to *Harrad*. I only wish I knew such vital and understanding people. You know, it is really a lonely path we are on—there are hoards of people, but, in my life anyway, few are willing to search beyond the eyes of themselves and others. In my earlier letter I mentioned friends who have read your book. It saddens me, though, because these same people who philosophized about it so enthusiastically have let their ideas slip into oblivion and continue as before the reading and discussions instead of using those ideas as stepping stones. But, the quest goes on for me—somewhat more lonely, but more knowingly.

And so, for sentimental Tomoff, your letter, book, and Christmas card mean much—but more than those are the thoughts behind them—Bob Rimmer. Thank you for all.

Sincerely,
Judith Tomoff
Oak Park, Michigan

August 2, 1967

Dear Mr. Rimmer:

I have recently read with profound interest your very provocative book *The Rebellion of Yale Marratt*. I should first like to say that I found the book stimulating, and not difficult reading. Your ideas and concepts as set forth in Marratt's short life are certainly not new. However, I do believe you have set them down with a measure of clarity such as has not been seen in these areas in the past.

Unless I am totally dense, *The Rebellion* sets forth the existentialist philosophy with only very slight modifications, to which I, personally, subscribe. I believe there are people who could easily fit into Yale Marratt's scheme, albeit, a pitifully small number. Thus, although ethically and/or philosophically Marratt's ideas are desirable, pragmatically they are nearly impossible. But be that as it may, I find myself philosophically pulling for Challenge, Inc., and the concepts it espouses.

I should like to study at greater length the Ten Commandments of Challenge, Inc. If you have them in some other form than as they appear in the book, I would appreciate your sending me a copy of them.

I realize that you are a busy author, however, I should be delighted to participate in a written dialogue of matters such as these. However, this would be dependent on the amount of your time you wish to spend with such matters.

Sincerely,
Zennen Ervin
Baltimore, Maryland

July 9, 1967

Dear Sirs,

In reference to *The Harrad Experiment* by Robert Rimmer, I would like to know if the Harrad Experiment actually took place. If the experiment did take place, is *The Harrad Experiment* by Robert H. Rimmer based on the facts from the journals of the students involved in the Harrad Experiment? If the experiment did take place, why is the book called "A novel by Robert H. Rimmer"? According to Webster's Unabridged Dictionary, the definition of a novel is:

A fictitious narrative (usually in prose) of some considerable length, representing human beings and their actions, etc ..."

If the Harrad Experiment didn't take place, is the

Introduction and editor's note a gimmick to convince or confuse the reader of the possible reality of the book.

I would appreciate a reply to my questions.

Thank you.

Sincerely,
Barry M. Nadell
Chicago, Illinois

July 23, 1968

Dear Mr. Rimmer:

I have just finished reading *The Harrad Experiment*, and to say the least, it is a most enlightening piece of work. It is hard to believe that such a school actually exists. It seems so idealistic on the one hand but then so right and necessary on the other.

Unfortunately, the bibliography is considerably limited in total number of volumes listed. Is it possible to obtain a listing of all the books covered in the Human Values Seminar? Your account has moved me to explore the situation at a deeper level.

Sincerely,
Mark Thomas Parrington
Norman, Oklahoma

October 13, 1967

Dear Mr. Rimmer,

This past week I had the pleasure of reading two of your books—*The Harrad Experiment* and *The Rebellion of Yale Marratt*. I was delighted because here it was—my philosophy in two books! I was beginning to think I was some kind of nut thinking the way I did, until I read your books.

A female friend and I (both of us are married and our husbands do not agree with the philosophy) have been discussing these ideas for several months but never could decide exactly where the religious ideas blended in with the sex ideas. I would like to read the books in your bibliography at the end of *The Harrad Experiment* but I doubt if I could obtain all of them, even though we have a well-stocked public library. My friend is now reading your books and I am looking forward to some very interesting discussions when she finishes. We were even thinking about collaborating on a book from the female point of view, and her having several husbands.

We both have a religious background of Unity, School of Practical Christianity, which stresses the goodness of man. But we have gone further both in our reading and believing with Yoga, ESP, psychic, Emerson, philosophy, psychology, and Hugh Hefner's philosophy. I guess we would be called "free thinkers." We believe that humans can love more than one mate and grow into better humans because of it.

If you have time I would appreciate an answer to a number of questions:

1. Are you writing any more books with similar themes?

2. Do you believe in the philosophy yourself?

3. Are you trying to change people's thinking by writing these books?

4. Have you received many letters from people who agree? Are there many, or aren't they admitting their beliefs?

5. Is there an organization in reality like Challenge, Inc.? If not, can you foresee an organization like it started? Are you interested in starting one?

6. Do you believe that people who believe in the philosophy of the books *can* begin to live this philosophy in their lives now, or do you think it is too far ahead of time?

I could ask many more questions and make many more comments but I won't take up your time. However, I do want to thank you for the books, for giving me the extreme pleasure of seeing my ideas actually in book form. For goodness sakes keep writing!

Sincerely yours,

Dear Mr. Rimmer,

Thank you for your letter of October 17. You answered my questions pretty well to my satisfaction, although HOW do you believe it is entirely feasible to personally live a life encompassing the philosophy that is presented in *Harrad* and in Challenge, Inc.? Wouldn't we be arrested with society the way it is? Maybe we could get away with living like that but we'd be living two different lives—one to keep from getting arrested and the other completely private. Wouldn't we be arrested for adultery (those of us who are married)? I've read a lot of ideas and not one book condones adultery. Even the *Playboy* philosophy and Albert Ellis advise against it. Now what?

I think I can tell you why you have appealed more to the female audience. The men in your stories tried to understand the women. They took the time to get to know them, to find out what they thought. They were sensitive without losing their masculinity—the type of man most women dream of knowing. Most men don't enjoy talking to women about beauty, joy, etc. I practically fell in love with Yale Marratt myself. To know a man like that would be pure heaven! If only men wouldn't think it was sissyish to discuss deep philosophical questions.

I would be very interested in having you send me some addresses of other females who obviously feel the same way I do. I love writing letters and discussing thoughts—of all kinds.

I am thirty-one and have an eight-year-old son. I have been married nine years. We live in a housing development (ugh) but would like to own an acre of land where we could have privacy. We are both high school graduates. My husband (the same age as I) is a typewriter repairman and I am a frustrated writer. (I had an article published in *Unity* magazine a year ago so can officially consider myself professional). I find I cannot write for the mass media because my thoughts are too far out for the general public and I can't write something I don't believe. So what I do is keep a journal where I write down all my deep and meaningful thoughts and experiences, complete with arguments I frequently have with myself on right and wrong, good and bad. I read a lot and hope someday to be able to write something meaningful. Right now I'm but a sponge—absorbing ideas, sifting out what I believe and don't believe, and trying to live as I believe one step at a time. I don't believe we belong in Vietnam; I don't believe in missionaries or charities or do-gooders. So you can see my ideas are kind of far out for the general public.

I just finished reading *Valley of the Dolls* because I wanted to see why it appealed to the masses. The book left me with a bad taste in my mouth and feeling very depressed. My neighbors are raving about it and I shudder because of all the meanness, shallowness, and petty jealousies in the book. Do people really identify with this type of book? Is this the mass appeal? Ugh! Let's have more love and respect in books—books that inspire and make you want to love your neighbor. Like your books! See, I'm an idealist too.

Yes, I heartily agree that we, in the next fifty years (maybe sooner), will have to care more about one another. This can come in no other way than getting to know each other more deeply. I read that a translation of *love* in the Bible is "understanding." When we understand God, or our neighbor, or ourselves, we will automatically love them.

I thoroughly believe that the only way we can help in this world is to *live* our philosophy but I don't know for sure if I have the nerve. Certainly I cannot love other men with a clear conscience without my husband's approval. We have had some discussions about this and he is beginning to open his mind. Yet would it work? Lord, I don't know. Sounds great in a book and in conversations—but in reality???

I am looking forward to your next book and fully intend to reread both *Harrad* and *Yale Marratt* so that I can get the philosophy imbedded in my mind.

Thank you again for taking the time to personally answer my letter and I will be looking forward to the addresses you send me. Should make interesting correspondences.

Sincerely yours,

Dear Mr. Rimmer.

I am sitting in the public library trying desperately to find reviews of *The Harrad Experiment.* I can find none and only enough on you to send this letter!

I am reviewing the book for "Book Group," a dozen or so young mothers most of whom went to Stanford ten years ago, before the changes in student life became so pronounced. There's no question that we will have an exciting evening!

If you would possibly have time to drop me a note soon after receiving this letter with answers to the thoughts outlined below, "Book Group" would be most appreciative.

Who was your Philip Tenhausen, the person with whom you discussed sex and life in order to come up with this philosophy of Human Values? (I had a feeling you were a sociology professor trying to popularize a favorite idea before I read your biography in *Contemporary Authors*).

Do you feel the ending, the group marriage and family-raising, is an inevitable result of shared roommates?

To you, is it a desired result for the people themselves and for society in general?

What led up to the writing of the *Experiment*? The trend of college students to live with each other in apartments off campus? The constant drive of young people in talk and hypocritical act to survive their sex drives? Or ——? Are your sons of an age to have influenced or have been influenced by this book?

Your answers and any reviews you might have would make for a clearer and more to-the-point evening for us.

P.S. Do you know about the Midpeninsula Free University, centered in the Palo Alto area? This last semester they offered a course (?) in the Harrad Experiment. I have yet to find out more.

Sincerely,
Karen B. Nilsson

Dear Mr. Rimmer:

Your letter was passed on to me by ———— when I expressed a desire for a class in "Human Values" at ———— University. ———— would like to see my husband and me accept the challenge of leading a class in human values.

We feel inadequate to lead such a class, as we have not yet had time to read all the books on your recommended reading list in the back of *The Harrad Experiment*. ———— suggested we write to you and ask if you have any ideas or suggestions to help us with this challenge. We do feel there is a definite need for this class, but we have only five weeks to prepare for the spring quarter.

I was very happy and surprised when ———— suggested I write to you. For oddly enough, there is no one I would rather meet than you. You see, I am my husband's second wife. He has been married to his first wife for eleven years, and we have been married for seven months. This happened before we even heard of Robert H. Rimmer.

We have all three read *The Harrad Experiment*, and ———— and I have read *The Rebellion of Yale Marratt*.

We were very pleased to have your new bibliography passed on to us. We are anxiously awaiting the printing of your new book. We are anxious to read both lists of books, for from what we have already read, we are better understanding our feelings.

Unfortunately, my sister-wife, ————, doesn't know the extent of our relationship. As with Anne and Cindar, I love her very much. Our husband, ————, and I want her to accept us more than any other thing. We want it to be an inclusive love and marriage rather than exclusive.

We wish that you could give us the answer to our problem, but realize that it would be difficult to do so.

———— and I are both attending the class "Sexual Morality Now" led by ———— and ————. One of the class's objectives is to break the path for ridding ourselves of jealousy in a relationship other than one to one. We are hoping to gain insight into ———'s feelings and to eliminate her fears.

Perhaps this is an area better described by ———.

I attended ———'s class "The Harrad Experiment." Unfortunately it fell apart. The class was divided into two groups—those desirous of a "free sex community" and those of us wanting a better way of life for us and our children.

Though we do not recommend our way of life to everyone (especially in its present state), we do feel that we should all be taught the value of Man, that is, Human Values. Any help you can give us would be deeply appreciated.

                   With respect and admiration,

                                 May 26, 1967

Dear Sir:

As I sit down to type this letter, I find myself so filled with warmth, and healthy, confusing thoughts, I hardly know where to begin. . . . I've just completed *The Harrad Experiment*!

We (my husband too) consider ourselves so extremely fortunate to have been able to share the beauty of *The Harrad Experiment* that we deeply thank you for giving us this gratifying experience.

Because your novel left us with such a fullness of life, we sincerely believe the man you named Philip Tenhausen does exist, and so we are asking for your help.

You see, *The Harrad Experiment* did vastly enrich our lives. Even though we personally were not educated in this manner, we desire to give this option of leading a full premarital life to our two girls.

How do we begin? We are not asking for exact names and details at this point due to consideration for your position and those involved. Therefore, we are willing to offer information concerning ourselves in such a manner as you suggest. (I hold a B.A. degree in history and Barry an M.A. degree in music. Barry comes from a Jewish home and I a Protestant home. Our main interests are drama and music.)

Please Mr. Rimmer, help us to find Philip and Margaret.

Thank you. . . .

Sincerely,

6 June 1967

Dear Mr. Rimmer,

"It gives me goose pimples to read it in a sense of identity—another person who thinks and feels the way I feel." (*The Harrad Experiment*, p. 144.)

I will be heading over to Syracuse (Upstate Medical Center) in July for a psychiatry residency. There, in a non-patient context, I hope to establish the sort of game-free transactional system envisioned in your novel.

Is there an opportunity for further communication?

Seth E. Many, M.D.

Dear Bob,

There is a furtive sense in me that this should be an Odd Essay. For if my initial letter induced a "warm chuckle," I must confess it was hopefully serious. And now (in order not to be a drag) I must avoid analyzing your friendly but ambivalent response. Perhaps this is epicritic? (still hopeful).

The last time I was posted a book it was *Taber's Medical Dictionary*. In gratitude I fatuously remarked that it would be of "lasting significance." (It has been lasting). I waver now between mere gratitude and gratitude plus fatuousness. But since history is gossip (or as Skinner might say, limited to esthetic value), I will make the plunge and thank you fully. For the rebellion of Yale Marratt is my own. It was in me (and you) before you wrote it. You wrote it. This is like discovering there are other people (conceit) on this crowded planet. Proud in our loneliness, this discovery of congruent individuality

114

infringes first the patents of self. Only later does the core being respond with extended visibility. Erikson claims that all relationships in life are defined by mutuality of function. But I don't think that it is mutuality which induces significance. This stems from the differences which persist within the context of mutuality. Mutuality is the precondition, allowing fear to dissipate (and me to write this). But mutuality without difference is static or regressive. Only difference permits re-perception. Thanks to you for *Yale*.

Existentially I am somewhere in part three, perhaps at the beginning of Chapter 5. There the problem of confrontation is met in vivo. The day is won by spontaneous emission. Saying this, I realize that I am only near the end of Chapter 4, for I have and do figurate a series of interrelationships, each of which is known and tolerated by the others. But, despite my anguished protest, they continue to embody the dualistic principle. Perhaps in the very process of this (unconscious) selection, the faithful are the jealous. Yet somehow I feel that it is not the non-commitment to the ideal (although that is sometimes manifest), but the non-commitment to me. But, I argue, charisma is person *plus*. And plus is total ecology. All of which is poor for mileage. The ultimately correct conditions are those which are successful. Where ideals are concerned all one can usually say is, "I must be doing something wrong!"

Finally, to sensualize a relationship is to bring it into the antianalytic, tribal, incorporative mode; to make of it being stuff. This I like. Yet we are also blessed with vision. Limitations legitimately imposed upon an interrelational system are those which result from systematic visualization, i.e. establishing functional objectives, specifying goals. Even in this latter sense I felt a strong contradiction in the Marratt consortium. The protective jealousy of two wives, in the face of a goal of mutual actualization, seemed far from graceful. At present, given our limited faculties of communication, it would seem that individual non-ritualistic intimacy is optimally attainable in small groups of six to eight persons. Nor can its function be zealously to guard the external boundaries from transgression and the internal borders from dissolution. Rather, full being is best elicited by free movement along a fluid continuum. This implies continued function within the larger community and the possibility, indeed the desirability, of continued movement to and from the essence group.

I just intoned most of this over the telephone to Carolyn, who is cramming for her bar exams in Syracuse. She enjoyed the pleasure I feel in its prospect of hope (and challenge). . . . Yoiks, are you a bit afraid of scaring me too?

Seth

P.S. I hope you have enough letters with permission to disclose identity and address, to strengthen the perceived reality of an actualized ideal.

Thursday, June 1, 1967

Dear Mr. Rimmer:

This is a sort of a fan letter. I've read two of your books, *The Harrad Experiment* and *The Rebellion of Yale Marratt*, and I've become very favorably disposed to the ideas and causes you raise in each one of them. I suppose as many people have told you, I wish I had gone to Harrad, or wish something like that had happened to me when I was in college. To compensate for that lack, I wonder if I should go out and marry two women . . . but that wasn't Yale Marratt's *intentional* plan, anyway. So I suppose I won't. Keeping up with one woman is bad enough. Unless two of them could start some kind of foundation, and support me more in the style to which I have become accustomed. Seriously, sir. I have enjoyed them both, as novels and as philosophical works. And if there's anything we under-twenty-five people can do to make such a healthy and sane world of dynamic love relationships a reality, I for one would like to lend a hand . . . both hands, with a lot of sweat, and hard work.

I read *The Harrad Experiment* in your friendly neighborhood paperback edition from Bantam. It was in that edition that I got this California address (Sherbourne Press) and decided to try and reach you there. Your paperback of *Harrad* has had surprisingly good distribution locally. One of the major newsstands has kept at least three or four copies of *Harrad* on its racks continuously since it went on sale in February or March. And these aren't the same copies. . . . They keep reordering due to healthy public demand. No, I've bought more copies than that, myself. I figure I've bought altogether at least five copies of *Harrad*, at ninty-five cents a crack. One I read, annotated, and underlined carefully. That's my personal copy. The second I gave to a friend on the occasion of his opening a bookstore-coffeehouse (something great locally), an agency for free thought and discussion. After reading the book, one night down there a friend, Paul Anderson, led a discussion of *The Harrad Experiment* with a group of young adults and college students, which I was unfortunately unable to attend. Two other copies of *Harrad* I loaned to people. ... I doubt if they'll ever give them up. And the fifth copy ... that I'm keeping hidden away in case of emergencies, such as other friends who might want to read it. I'm sure your royalties are generous—it's a very fine, very valuable book.

After still another friend of mine, a young woman from Rockford named Tory Schulz, read your *Harrad Experiment*, she wrote you a letter and sent it to the Sherbourne Press address. In reply, you wrote her and sent her a hardcover copy of *The Rebellion of Yale Marratt*, published by Challenge (wonderful coincidence) Press. It was this copy she has passed to several friends as I have passed around *Harrad*. I guess you must be responsible for producing some kind of "underground" books—at least they seem to be breeding a secret alliance of conspirators for sanity. I was the latest to read Mrs. Schulz's copy of *Yale Marratt*—she just came over to the house last night to reclaim it for another friend, the day after I finished reading it.

I have read somewhere—in some publisher's list, although now I can't track it down—that on the strength of your popular success with *Harrad*, a paperback edition of *Yale Marratt* had been published, under the aegis of Avon books, for 95 cents. It seems like only a month ago that I read of this event in the "New Books Published" list of the arch-puritan Chicago *Sunday Tribune*, which obviously didn't know what it was promoting. (They removed Elia Kazan's *The Arrangement* from the best-seller list because they *did* read that and didn't approve of it.)

Hollywood would really have a shit fit trying to convert one of your social documents into their usual homogenized, hygienic product. Yale Marratt would turn into a kindly old man like Amos Tangle who had an abiding love for two daughters; his Challenge farms would produce milk; and even the "gadfly" button would have to be dropped, no doubt, because some people associate "fly" with phallic symbolism. No, I'm afraid movies are one "art" form that isn't brave or honest enough to serve as vehicles for thought, your thought anyway. That's one brand of popular success you'll probably have to do without. Although I continue to have hope—I was very favorably impressed with the honest and straightforward treatment Joseph Strick gave in filming James Joyce's *Ulysses*. It's a beautiful film, not a bit "dirty" despite the frankness of Joyce's language, which was preserved intact in many sequences. But if many critics hadn't trumpeted for it and made it kind of a sacred cow in America, I wonder if it wouldn't have been banned, confiscated, or illegally scissored at various locations around our liberal homeland.

It's nothing now for movies, even the popular clump, to show a bit of nudity or speak a flavorful word. Now I only hope they become adult enough to start treating serious movie themes without flinching. Sexploitation and voyeurism are the products of the society that outwardly practices "morality" in the hands of hatchet-wielding grandmothers. The expletives in *Virginia Woolf* supposedly paved the way for something—probably for more expletives. I'd like to see, however, a courageous and uncompromising filmization of something controversial—like *The Last of the Just* or *The Harrad Experiment*.

How did I get onto this subject? What I wanted to say was—now that I've given it back to Mrs. Schulz, I no longer have any copy of *Yale Marratt*. And I have nothing but paperback editions of *Harrad*. I would like to obtain permanent, hard-bound copies of all three of your published novels so far—*Harrad*, *Yale Marratt*, and the earlier *That Girl from Boston*, of which I know nothing but the title. I'd also like to get "on your mailing list"— be advised whenever you have something new that's about to come out. As a novelist-crusader-philosopher, you are one of my favorite writers, and I'd like to assemble something of a complete personal library of your writings— books, stories, articles, speeches, newspaper interviews, what have you. Would it be possible, first of all, to buy hardcover copies of the three books directly from you? Please let me know, and let me know what the price would be. A number of my friends have been prodding me to write to you as their spokesman, too. So I said I would, as soon as I finished reading *Yale Marratt*.

Oh—who am I? I'm a newspaper reporter, age twenty-three, with two years of college behind me at the University of Wisconsin. Someday I'll have to go back and get a degree in drama. I work for two weekly newspapers in suburban Loves Park, north of Rockford—*The Post*, which comes out on Thursdays; and the *Monday Morning Mail*, which of course is published on Mondays. I write sports, entertainment, play reviews, police and court news, civic and governmental news, features, social events, church bulletins—and take pictures—till it's coming out of my ears. But I try to keep an independent and active mind.

Thank you for making me think, and providing some good reading pleasure in the bargain. In the back of the Bantam edition of *Harrad* it says: "Mr. Rimmer describes himself as a writer who thinks he can move the world, and he is busily trying to find a place to put the fulcrum." How about planting it close to Rockford? I am sure you could find a lot of sympathetic vibrations here among people who are fed up with the restrictive stereotypes, prejudices, provincialities, and prohibitions of our little up-tight reactionary Rockford.

I'm looking forward to hearing from you.

Sincerely,
Bill Loudin
Rockford, Illinois

Sept. 20, 1967

Dear Mr. Rimmer,

I have recently been invited by the U.K. Student Forum committee to participate in a roundtable type discussion of *The Harrad Experiment*. I am honored to be selected for the panel concerning what, I can honestly say, has been one of the major influences on my thinking.

In order to be prepared for the forum there are two questions which I'd like to have answered. Neither concerns the philosophy within the novel, but rather are interested in the pragmatic policy presented to put the ideal society into practice.

First, I have a question about the labor pool. If, under the educational system, everyone in the state of X has the opportunity to attend either college or trade school, who does that leave to do the menial jobs so necessary for a society's functioning? What I'm wondering is where the janitors, garbage men, assembly-line workers, and the like will come from? It seems that they will have to be drawn from the mentally deficient, thus bogging down the economic system of the state and dooming the "reformer" politicians to defect.

Second, and more important, is the question of being able to condition the young to a new value system. How is the educational system going to be able to offset the teaching of parents and unsympathetic clergy. Surely there will be a vast number of adults who will refuse to listen to, let alone consider, the new value system. What is to keep them from conditioning their children to the prejudices and jealousies which mark our society today? It's obvious that people, opposed to the Harrad ideals, could cause enough pressure to crumble the entire system.

Answers to these two questions would make me feel fully prepared to well represent your views, as I understand them, on the panel in middle October.

One more thing: I read that *Harrad* is being made into a movie. Please don't let Hollywood turn it into a run-of-the-mill sensationalistic teen-age love/sex story. Don't let them turn the story into something it's not and leave out what the book is really about.

Thank you very much for your time.

Sincerely,
Douglas Morrison
Lexington, Kentucky

22 March 1967

Dear Mr. Rimmer:

Have just finished reading your novel, *The Harrad Experiment* and am very impressed.

There are many aspects of life today which modern man has much contempt for, and on an average, he has the ability of doing nothing about the way of the suppressing of his feelings and emotions by society.

In your novel, I have the feeling that you are trying to do something about a few of these many aspects—love, sense of security, true feelings and emotions, and many others interwoven into these basics.

I do not condone all the means you portrayed to reach the end in your novel; I will also say I do not believe you were writing a novel form of your philosophy. I think you are making great steps for the natural way.

Again, let me express my appreciation of your fine novel; I am anxiously awaiting your next.

Sincerely,
William G. Graves
Brooklyn, New York

March 13, 1967

Dear Sir,

I have just finished your novel *The Harrad Experiment*. I have not only enjoyed it, I am involved with it. The concept of living that you have advocated has taken hold of me and I cannot shake it off, even if I wanted to. I must know if this is a fiction of your imagination or an account of a true experiment. If it is a creation of your own, may I congratulate you on a fine mind and an enviable style of writing. If this concept belongs to another (i.e., Phillip Tenhausen), I would be grateful if you would send me his address so that I may satisfy my interest in the matter. Enclosed is a pre-addressed, stamped envelope.

Yours gratefully,
Burleigh Angle

Dear Mr. Rimmer,

I am extremely sorry that I have taken so long to answer your letter and to thank you for your very kind gift. However, the first thing I wanted to do was to read *The Rebellion of Yale Marratt*. That in itself took a good bit of time, as I had to keep up with my studies at the same time. Also, I have been working in a production of the musical *Carnival*.

But this is all extraneous material, which is just a waste of your time. You will be pleased to know that *The Harrad Experiment* has become a very great topic of discussion. Since I bought my copy, I have seen many people on campus reading it. I no longer know where my own copy is, as it has been passed from hand to hand.

I have talked with many people about it and have gotten a few good ideas out of it all. One of the most interesting came from a divinity student at Ohio Wesleyan. His thought was to combine the ideas of *The Harrad Experiment* with the ideas on the new secular religion, *The Secular City* by Harvey Cox (being the best book on the topic that I know of that is of recent publication). To be truthful, I have not gone beyond the discussion stage in my research into the idea, but from this great amount of talking, I feel that the position of the Harrad ideals would be greatly enhanced by such a coordination of forces.

Now that I think back upon *The Harrad Experiment* I feel sure that it is not such a great revolution as it might seem at first. The Harrad philosophy is in reality in progress at Berkeley, Yale, Harvard, etc. Though I do not actively participate in such activities as the free sex movement, I do feel that it is the beginning of a new recognition of the value of mankind. The Harrad idea is an evolutionary movement. As the present youth of America grow older, they will realize that the most important part of life is the education that they will need—not just education to become successful, but also education in human values. As Camus put it, man is a stranger in a society that desires to make each person act in a prescribed manner, but with the evolution of the Harrad ideal, man will no longer be a stranger, and that society will be based on the concept of allowing the individual to live life to his fullest capacity, in hopes that man can achieve a continual union with nature, the earth, the universe, even unto the greater presence of God's mind.

Yours in thanks,
Burleigh P. Angle
Sewickley, Pennsylvania

July 31, 1967

Dear Sir,

I have just completed reading your publication *The Harrad Experiment* and am tremendously engrossed with the ideas and philosophy therein. The Introduction leaves me in doubt as to the actual existence of Margaret and Phillip Tenhausen. Since I believe that the concepts the book contains would be of tremendous interest at the medical school with which I am affiliated, I would like to invite these people to our school to speak—if there are such people as the Tenhausens.

If it is at all possible would you be so kind as to inform me where I might get in touch with the Tenhausens and the author, Robert Rimmer. I believe it would be a most exciting experience to expose both the students and faculty at Albert Einstein College of Medicine to this revolutionary approach to education and to discuss its sociological and developmental implications with the individuals involved.

I trust you will be able to help me so I thank you in advance for your time and effort in my behalf. I eagerly await your answer.

Sincerely,
Alvin S. Blaustein
Bronx, New York

Sept. 8, 1967

Dear Mr. Rimmer,

I was most pleased and excited to receive your letter. Frankly, I was not too surprised that "Harrad" was not in existence. This doesn't, however, dim the enthusiasm with which I received the thoughts forwarded in your book. By this time, I have already had many opportunities to discuss with my peers some of your ideas and methods. Needless to say, there has been somewhat less than complete agreement. Many people are still imprisoned by traditional beliefs, refusing to realize the personal fulfillment possible by a more realistic approach to education. Others, myself included, recognize some change is necessary but do not find your ultimate conclusions congruent with what we consider to be our "democratic" heritage. This does not, however, detract in the least from the merit of your speculative plans but merely indicates that your book has succeeded in provoking a great deal of both personal introspection and examination of our society as it stands.

A letter, of course, is no place to discuss ideas. The written word is too easily miscomprehended and does not necessarily convey the desired thought. I would, on behalf of the Student Council here at Albert Einstein College of Medicine like to invite you to our school. I don't know what your usual arrangements are, but I would be most happy to do my best to see that they are fulfilled. The visit and exchange would, of course, be at your convenience. Please let me know if such a visit is possible and what I must do at this end to facilitate it.

I look forward to hearing from you. And thank you so much for forwarding me your other novel.

Sincerely,
Alvin Blaustein

February 20, 1967

Dear Sir:

I don't know how well you've succeeded in moving the rest of the world, but you've done quite well with me. I am now in the process of reading as many of the books you listed in *The Harrad Experiment* as possible. I had already read Maslow's *Toward a Psychology of Being* and I managed to find a copy of A. S. Neill's *Summerhill, A Radical Approach to Child Rearing*. Some books I've ordered and some I can't because you didn't mention any publishers.

Sad as it may seem, I'm a twenty-three-year-old still in the process of formulating a philosophy of life. But then, I've always been slow. Perhaps I should damn you for giving me food for thought. Why? Once I have formulated my views, I know it will be almost impossible for me to find a woman (or girl?) who shares them. The world is so big and I'm just one person—a person still not sure just what he wants to do in life.

I've got a B.S. degree in chemistry and I don't know what I want to be. I look out at the world and wonder how I fit into a place when I agree with so little of what's being said. I could follow the usual path, but I'd hate myself for the rest of my life. I look out at some of our staunch patriots and wonder. I don't feel that the world owes me a living, but I don't feel that I owe my country my life either.

But I'm getting ridiculous. I don't even know that you'll get this letter. And if you do, you probably won't read it. I'll close by saying that I wish there were a Harrad and that I could have gone there. Perhaps then I wouldn't feel so alone.

Sincerely,
Gordon G. Broussard
College Station, Texas

August 7, 1967

Dear Mr. Rimmer,

I am writing in response to your book *The Harrad Experiment*. Your book has made a vivid impression on all of us who have read it. Most of us have read nine or ten books on the Harrad bibliography and are obtaining more of the suggested books at the present time. For the past three months, our readings have been the main topic of conversation and due to this we have organized a discussion group just for this purpose. We are all in agreement that the ideas and attitudes expressed in *Harrad* seem to be more healthy than the prevalent attitudes of our present society. Due to our active acceptance of many of the theories from our reading, we are planning to enroll in a class on "Interpersonal Relationships and Sensitivity Training."

Because of the questions I plan to ask in behalf of our group, it will be to our benefit to have you know the

125

following facts about our group. We are three married couples, ages twenty-four to twenty-nine, all active professionally. Among us are two registered nurses, an engineer, a teacher, a doctoral candidate in pathology, and a vice-president of a northwest lumber concern.

1. Was this experiment actually initiated?

    a. If so, where and by whom?

    b. If so, is it possible for us to correspond with this individual?

2. Since there is no *North American Journal of Sociology*, if there was a report, in what periodical was it published?

3. Or is this book a product of your own imagination and convictions?

4. To your knowledge, has a Harrad program been initiated in the U.S. since the book was published? If so, how successful has it been?

5. If there actually is a group putting the Harrad theories into practice, would it be possible for you to arrange for us to correspond with them?

6. As the year progresses we would like to correspond with you as our minds compose more questions. Also, if possible, during your travels or ours, we would like to arrange a meeting to pursue your theories further.

7. As we consume more reading material—the need for additional Human Values selections is evident. We hope you may make more suggestions to complete our readings. Your indulgence in this respect would be appreciated.

Sincerely,

August 17, 1967

Dear Mr. Rimmer,

After a short conversation with Kay, my thoughts and reactions seemed to crystallize, and along with my adrenalin screaming for release, not maliciously but anxiously.

First of all, the idea proposed by *Harrad* that made the deepest impression on me was the intimate relationship (total, not just sexual) achieved between two people who were not man and wife. The reason this appeals to me is that I feel Mike (my husband) and I have an exceptional total relationship, *but* I do not think it is possible for any one person to be always perceptive of another's emotional and intellectual needs.

I don't believe that this plan could possibly be achieved by married individuals unless they have been able to break down moral, sex taboos, jealousy and communicative barriers, and in the process become emotionally secure.

May I say that if nothing ever comes of our discussions and letters, a great deal will have been gained through them. That, being personal insight into another's emotions and personality. All of us have achieved this to a certain degree along with helping to stabilize one another's emotional security. Besides, it is a very exciting idea to imagine ourselves as pioneers in communal marriage. But before we can proceed in this direction, we have a great many enigmas to solve.

1. Mike and I have four preschool children and as many problems as possible must be solved before we draft a plan of action.

2. The legal aspect of communal marriage in *Harrad* was, for me, inadequately covered. By living in a communal marriage situation we would open ourselves to possible and probable problems with law enforcement agencies, especially since there are children involved. There are many laws we would be subject to and breaking those laws could result in a number of things: (a) loss of children, (b) imprisonment for being lewd persons and contributing to the delinquency of a minor, (c) loss of professional positions, (d) children and adults ostracized by society. There will always be people who disapprove of our way of life. At present, we don't see a way to resolve this situation or see any way to prevent this sequential progression. ON THIS WE COULD CERTAINLY USE SOME PRACTICAL SUGGESTIONS!

Goal: COMMUNAL LIVING—Since I feel our marriages are much better than most, and because of this and the children involved, none of us have the desire to jeopardize our marriages for these views. Consequently, at this time, it seems highly dangerous to pursue sexual interests, mainly because we are not all at the same level of acceptance. My own thoughts are that intellectual interest and promise of intellectual and domestic compatibility are of more importance, along with a small amount of physical attraction, than sexual compatibility. Sexual compatibility should follow spontaneously. A unanimity of goals and standards seems evident and necessary.

Please feel free to challenge or point out any fallacies in my thoughts and reactions. By giving you a little insight into my thoughts and reactions, I hope you may be able to offer solutions that we may have overlooked.

We all were pleased to read your interesting and inspiring letter and hope to receive more. I'll not thank you for the bibliography because I don't have it—so, fire away with the questions or I'll be needing the list before you're prepared to release it.

Sincerely,

P.S. (For Kay) Are you currently corresponding with any other groups contemplating marriage? If so, are their reactions and conflicts similar or different than ours?

Sept. 13, 1967

Dear Mr. Rimmer,

As we have not received a reply to our letter of approximately August 17, '67, I decided to drop a letter to make sure you didn't feel we weren't worth the time. We have been anxiously awaiting your reaction to our letter and in the meantime we have formulated another letter. There have been many developments and changes of attitude since our last correspondence. We found your letter encouraging, as we sometimes are and were lacking perspective.

The books arrived a few days after we mailed the last letter. I have just finished *The Rebellion of Yale Marratt*. I found it a *beautiful* (not loosely) story, not because of the fictional material but for the ideas. I felt a bit uneasy on seeing the autograph at the front of the book. But, during the past few weeks the word LOVE has begun to mean something very different to all of us and *With Love* meant that you are and do live your philosophy of life. Thank you for sending them.

I am *still* reading *Toward a Psychology of Being*. This book has been very meaningful to me as well as inspiring.

Sincerely with affection,

May 27, 1968

Dear Bob,

I have thought of you many times these past nine months; several times I have written but never revised the letter—so today I decided to let it be spontaneous and forget about revisions.

All of us here have changed a great deal, but communal living is a thing of the "closet." Mainly because Ken and Mike do not have the convictions to carry the project—they are still very hampered by the societal structure. But yet, their religious and moral views have been liberalized a great deal. Maybe Kay and I are at the advantage by reading and discussing more. Needless to say, there has been a very strong bond developed between the four of us. This has been a rough year for all four of us as (1) Ken and I have just completed our masters' programs, (2) Mike has been working twenty extra hours a week, (3) Kay is expecting a baby (Kay has been particularly unstable as she has never carried a fetus to term), (4) My starting to actualize (some) has caused no end of problems in our marriage, and consequently we have been in counseling since February. We were in counseling before Mike and I realized that all of our conflicts were not due to growth pains. So, thank God, we seem to be making some progress. This summer, Mike and I are auditing a contemporary philosophy seminar which will offer more opportunity for growth.

It has been very painful to watch a man whom I love dearly stay behind, many times due to fear. Especially as I feel it is impossible to walk back through the door experientially. I get quite emotional just writing to you about it—I guess because I fear that unless something happens to give Michael the drive toward personal growth we will end up separated. Right now, I feel as though Mike is asking me to suppress a need for experience, achievement, conviction, as well as individuality, for something he feels secure with—the traditional American housewife. So this is what happens when all don't feel the need to *expand their horizons*. (Can you offer any suggestions here?)

Mike and I have been involved in sensitivity labs and I found it very rewarding. Mike found the experience exhilarating—temporarily. The ability I gained toward being outgoing and open has enhanced my interpersonal relationships immensely.

I am still doing lots of reading—right now *The Outsider* (Colin Wilson), *Gestalt Therapy* (Perls), *On Becoming a Person* (Carl Rogers), *This Is It* (Alan Watts).

How is your book coming on communal marriage? Intentional community? I've been watching for it.

I'm hoping to make a week at Esalen—at Big Sur, California—by Christmas. I suppose you've heard about Esalen—the super-sensitivity institute.

If you happen to ———, please call. We all would enjoy seeing and talking to you. If you've never been here, you should visit; it is beautiful country.

I have enjoyed many times over the extra effort put into your Christmas card. This has not only been meaningful to me but to friends.

I considered enclosing some other correspondence but didn't know if you would be interested.

Your return letter will be anxiously awaited.

With Love,

July 13, 1969

Dear Mr. Rimmer,

I am writing as the Editor of *SOLEM*, the University of Manchester's student magazine, to say how interesting I found your book *The Harrad Experiment*. It was sent out as a review copy to publications such as mine, and I was invited to a press reception on 4th July. I would very much like to have met you then to talk a little about the ideas you expressed in your book, but unfortunately, I was not able to stay in Manchester till then.

However, as I am thinking of including an article on your book in the magazine—an article that would be more substantial than a review—I was wondering if you could possibly write me something about the sociological ideas you express in the novel. Although the presentation of the book would not lead one to suspect the serious intent of its subject matter, I find the whole very interesting. The fact that its commercial appeal, as a paperback, will sell millions of copies, and therefore millions of readers will be exposed to this stimulating thinking, is in itself, interesting.

May I ask, first of all, if there is any truth in the experiment, or is it all wishful thinking? Regardless of truth or not, the bibliography of the ideas form a very sound basis for such an attitude to life. The book, it seems to me, has certainly appeared at an exciting time, for today with emphasis on the Californian hippie culture, where L.S.D. breaks down the old social formulae and replaces them by the ideal of love, your experiment approaches the transition in a much more intelligent, profound and humane way—one that is closely related to human beings as they are. Such new thinking is very exciting and is perhaps the best way to cope with the changes experienced today. I should, therefore, be very grateful if you could spare some time to write down such ideas in a straightforward, reasoned way, so that an article based on these ideas could be included in the magazine. An alternative would be possible if you could give us permission to reprint large chunks of your novel, verbatim. I am sure that you would find our magazine interesting and stimulating, for our aim is merely to deal with as wide a scope of ideas, as objectively as possible. And I assure you that students in Manchester will find your sociological ideas fascinating, not as mere sexual titillation, but as a new and deeply considered attitude to life.

I look forward to hearing from you as soon as possible, and remain,

Yours sincerely,
Miss Carol M. Dix
Manchester, England

April 4, 1968

Dear Sir:

A friend gave me a copy today of *The Harrad Experiment* by Robert H. Rimmer. I read the book at one sitting and was fascinated and genuinely interested in the ideas of Margaret and Phillip Tenhausen. I am writing to ask whether or not these people are real, or an integral part of Rimmer's fiction. The Introduction implies that they are real people and that Harrad College, though a pseudonym, exists. Yet the title calls the book a novel, a work of fiction. Is the Introduction also a part of the fictional literary vehicle that Rimmer has used to express his ideas?

I would appreciate an answer to these questions, since, if the Tenhausens are real people, I would like to pursue my acquaintance with them and their ideas further.

Thank you for your trouble.

Yours truly,
Paul Davern
Ottawa, Canada

Dear Mr. Rimmer:

You have doubtless received volumes of mail concerning *The Harrad Experiment*, but I sincerely hope you have time to answer this one.

First, a question that must've been asked by a million people: Was Harrad College a fact? If so, why was the book presented as a "Novel by Robert H. Rimmer"?

I hope it was a fact. Such an experiment is desperately needed if it hasn't happened, and needs national repetition if it has.

You might be interested to know that the Midpeninsula Free University offers a course entitled "The Harrad Experiment," in which the group is encouraged to examine Harrad principles and evolve their own relationships in an unrestricted manner. I hope to be able to take the course in the Spring Quarter.

If Harrad College was a fact, what success if any was experienced by the InSix in their infiltration of a state's political system? If that's not privileged information, that is.

And also, if Harrad was a fact, is there any way of contacting the administrators involved? I am twenty-five years old and have personally evolved similar relationships with several people, though my adjustment (without the benefit of Harrad) was a period of chaotic trauma for me. I would like to work for such a society of people, and I hope to return to school soon for my degree in Psychology. My I.Q. (at last count) was 148.

Would you send me the mailing address of Harrad College, or perhaps to preserve security, would you give them my name and address? I honestly believe such a community is the only hope for mankind. Thank you very much.

Sincerely,
Donald L. Cline
Mountain View, California

May 24, 1968

Dear Mr. Rimmer,

Five minutes ago I finished *The Rebellion of Yale Marratt*. Last summer I read *The Harrad Experiment*. I thoroughly enjoyed both of them, and your heroes are the first I have been able to identify with in American fiction since *Atlas Shrugged*.

Does either Challenge, Inc., or Harrad exist? I will graduate from Duke University in ten days with a degree in zoology and no place in particular to go. What can I do to help implement these ideas?

Sincerely,
Bill Wallace,
Washington, North Carolina

September 6, 1967

Dear Mr. Rimmer,

We have just finished reading *The Harrad Experiment* and we know that the new hope for life it has given us will last a long time. We have been married two and one half years, have two children and have been living with an ever-present and growing fear that we are alone or very nearly alone in our struggle to give ourselves and our children a climate of love and life-affirming existence. We presently live in a suburban community and are of course, dissatisfied. We have both been working on a part-time basis to further our academic status because it has been our impression that living in the academic atmosphere surrounding a liberal university might be an improvement. Although we still believe that this is probably so, we have lately become convinced that very often intellectuals do not continue to exercise because of a desire to reaffirm life through enlightenment and experience, but instead, they burden themselves with mental labor because it helps them to divorce themselves from their lives, which they find painful. This realization has placed a doubt in our minds concerning the merit of turning to academia for the answer.

What we are saying is that we have been striving for life, indeed struggling for life, and in our inarticulate way we have known all along what we have wanted for ourselves and our children. But your book has formed words out of our stammering, and we shall be eternally grateful to you for having come into our lives.

On the last page in *The Harrad Experiment* a note stated that you think you can move the world. If by this you mean you will move it through your writing, you have succeeded in moving two more people. If you mean that you intend to take some more concrete action, you now have two more disciples who are tired of fighting alone and who would like to help, and be helped. Count us in!

Victor and Carole Garlock
Auburn, New York

September 21, 1967

Dear Mr. Rimmer,

Thank you so much for the copy of *The Rebellion of Yale Marratt* which you sent us. We were surprised and delighted to receive both it and your letter.

My husband is heavily loaded with reading the psychology books necessary for him to obtain his master's degree next June and has not been able to read *Yale Marratt* yet, although he is anxious to get to it. I have just finished reading it and cannot contain my enthusiasm long enough to wait so that we may write to you together again. Vic understands and says he will add his comments when he has read it.

As I read *Yale Marratt* I found the human quality of the characters fantastic considering the idealistic basis of the story. Reading this book is truly a growth experience. I lived Yale's quest for meaning, love, joy and life as I read. I have read a great many novels, but never before have I been so caught up and stirred.

I believe that the concept of man expressed by Yale, as I understand it, is ultimately true, but that man now is

134

a product of what has gone before him and that he will not allow this product to be destroyed because it is all he knows of himself. Yale felt a burning desire to show his fellowmen the way to achieve life—he couldn't be content to just experience it himself. If this were real life, I think I know how his trial for bigamy would come out; it seems as if people are driven to destroy what they don't understand.

It seems to me that if we love man we cannot ignore the bogey men he lives with, the fears and needless confinements he protects himself with. If we try to strip him of these and show him something better, he will strike out. The idea expressed in *The Harrad Experiment* to take over a state, and gradually, but firmly and dynamically, reeducate the people to accept love and the divinity of man seems to me to be a really workable plan. Unlike the bombshell of Challenge, Inc., it would not immediately excite the loud voices of fear. Instead of reaching the flexible few capable of thinking outside the confines of their experience, it would provide experiences and pave the way for growth toward the ideas necessary, I think, to man if he is to survive. Surely we could try to live what we know is right within our sphere and perhaps influence those whom chance thrusts near us, but I can't help feeling that the world is our sphere, and if we don't actively try to influence it we will be consumed by loneliness for the brotherhood of all men.

You, Mr. Rimmer, are widely read and have experienced a great deal more than I; do you believe it possible to attempt to follow a plan to help people achieve a society actively working to live by the Ten Commandments of Challenge, Inc.?

Mr. Rimmer, thank you once again for sending us your book and letter, but most of all thank you for writing your books.

Sincerely,
Carole Garlock
Auburn, New York

February 9, 1967

Dear Mr. Rimmer,

To the numerous accolades which you have doubtless received for your novel *The Harrad Experiment*, permit me to add my own diminutive conviction that you have surely created *momentum aere perennius*.

After reading (and subsequently, rereading) the text, experiencing with unabashed delight the dulcet harmonies of interpersonal development, I found myself continually drawn to the conclusion that the description of incident and motivating circumstance was simply too consistently flexuous to be creative portrayal. Rather, it must be the result of a compassionate assemblage of highly individual, but related, autobiographies. If I am incorrect in my assumption—which is only too probable—you are to be doubly complimented. However, if I have decided rightly, even in part, perhaps this world of ours is a bit less lonely and sterile than I have found it.

Somehow, my wife and I have yet to discover a person who has succeeded in breaching his inner, walled city of intellectual and emotional excellence. Our acquaintances, most of whom are technically disciplined (I am an engineering-physicist), tend inevitably to be educated, literate, and barren. It may be that the above notion is no more than the expression of a *need* to believe that man is really capable of self-realization.

Fortunately, whether or not we finally achieve the fundamental pleasure of truly sharing this curious irritation called life with another empathetic being, we will have nevertheless become richer for the knowledge that such a person does, indeed, exist.

My deepest regards,

February 12, 1968

Dear Mr. Rimmer,

I have read with interest the two books you wrote entitled *The Harrad Experiment* and *The Rebellion of Yale Marratt*.

I enjoyed the reading of them very much, but even more than that, they seemed to touch on problems which are continually coming up in the area of counseling which I get involved in. I suspect this to be true on a wide scale for any minister. I am not sure what reaction these books would bring from other ministers or even from my own superiors. I have not discussed them with others in the clergy, but for me they have been helpful.

My reason for writing is that I am interested in reading the other book you wrote entitled *That Girl from Boston*. I cannot find it at any bookstore in the area and thought perhaps you could tell me a source for it. I would appreciate any suggestion you might be willing to make.

Yours very truly,

The Original Introduction to The Harrad Experiment

Sometimes authors caught up in their own enthusiasms need editors. Had I had my way *The Harrad Experiment* would have been titled *Experiment in Marriage* and the original Introduction would have been in two sections, with the material that follows presumably an actual evening with Phillip and Margaret Tenhausen. Quite possibly the publisher was right on both scores. My original title sounds a little like a marriage manual, and the length might have put-off the reader who wanted to get to the story. But among other things, the original Introduction does raise the question all of us must face. Can a democratic society, which still is in the throes of absorbing the explosion of a hundred million people in the past thirty years, cope with and give a sense of purpose to an additional hundred million people in the next thirty years? Or does the very nature of the people dilution create vast arenas of minor petty conflicts making it impossible for the majority to unite on anything except mediocrity? My own feeling is that if democracy in the form we now have it is going to survive, we must elect leaders who have the vision to lead and *dare* to lead. In the process we will move always slightly to the left of center, with the left being a fuller life experience for all men.

RETROSPECT

Six months ago when John Carnsworth asked if I would be interested in working with Phillip and Margaret Tenhausen on this first report on the Harrad College Premarital Living Program, I recalled the first evening that Phil and Margaret had discussed the proposal with a group of students in their apartment that overlooks the Charles River in Boston. I remembered that Margaret had let the tape recorder run. "I'm not doing it to capture your undying thoughts," she told us, "but after years of marriage I have discovered that often Phil is at his best when he gets ranting in a group. Some of his ideas are tenuous and I like to go back and re-examine them later."

After reading more than thirty-two separate and several composite journals maintained by the first graduates of Harrad over a period of four years, I suggested to Phil that while his introduction to the journals we had selected was precise and to the point, as I remembered that evening four years ago there was a conversational give and take that might help the reader gain a better understanding of the program. We listened to the tape, which incidentally was now in the possession of John Carnsworth, and Phil agreed to let me use it in any way I saw fit. Since it raises, and since it contains in one section Phil at his raving, ranting best, an intellectual delight which will be familiar to all Harrad students, I have interpolated this tape to try and give the reader the feeling of that evening.

All of us who were at the Tenhausens that evening were working at various colleges and universities in the Boston area on grants from the Carnsworth foundation. Attracted by the international fame of the Tenhausens and revelling in the world of ideas, all of us considered the opportunity to be at one of the Tenhausens' gatherings an exceptional privilege.

As is her custom Margaret served us each a glass of Liebfraumilch ... "to stimulate our thinking" and announced with a little grin that she and Phil were embarking on a project that might eventually have wider repercussions for mankind than the hydrogen bomb.

Sitting indolently in his worn leather chair, one leg over its arm, Phillip Tenhausen looked at us seriously through hornrimmed glasses that were much too large for his thin face. He flipped several hundred pages of a typewritten manuscript, and said, "This is our final report to the Carnsworth Foundation. Before I tell you in detail about it, I thought it might be fun and somewhat enlightening to do a little research among graduate students and Ph.D's who have already been through the mill of their undergraduate days and survived quite well from the looks of all of you.

"As you know, Margaret and I have been working for several years in the area of pre-marital sexual relations not only among college students but among all teen-agers." He chuckled. "None of you here are any longer teen-agers and yet among the five couples here, all of whom are now in their late twenties, only you ... Bob and Erma are married ... so to all intents and purposes although you are all in your middle twenties, sexually (except for one married couple) you are at the same impasse as any beginning freshman in college.

"Before I explain the Harrad program in detail I must ask that you keep the entire discussion this evening ... How do the politicians say it? 'Off the record.' We are not looking for publicity. However, since all of us have been well acquainted for some years I know that you are going to hear rumors about what the Tenhausens are doing. This evening is not to dispel the rumors, simply to quell them a little for you." Phillip paused. "Let me approach the Harrad project by doing a little personal probing into your lives. If my questions get too personal you can plead the fifth amendment." He turned to me.

"Bob, you are about twenty-seven years old ... think back to your freshman days in college. You didn't know Erma then did you?"

Erma was sitting on the floor propped against my legs. We had married the year before, just after I had landed a job with the Carnsworth Foundation.

"I didn't know Erma when I was eighteen. I was scared to death of girls, and I had acne."

"That's not true." Erma laughed. "He was engaged to someone else in college."

Phillip smiled. "How was your sex life, Bob?"

"Very erratic, and usually more worry than fun."

"Then girls were very much a part of your mental life."

139

"That's right, Phil ... incessantly. Very nice day-dreaming with very little solid substance."

"Did you think about boys when you were eighteen, Erma?"

"Continuously ... but I don't get the point," Erma said. "Every normal girl and boy reacts the same. You are simply pointing up the obvious, Phil. At a certain age boys become a number one pre-occupation for girls and vice versa."

"And in the United States it continues to be ... not a pre-occupation, perhaps," Tom Willton, a graduate instructor in psychology, interjected. "But certainly an avocation for the average male well into middle age. Look around you. Our mass entertainment which occupies most of our leisure (or escape from the dull routine of living in an industrial society) is largely sex-oriented. The average American male and female obviously are sexually frustrated, or they wouldn't respond so well. I have a friend who insists that with a little clever psychology to release her, it would be possible for him to climb in the sack with practically any female who has been married ten or more years."

"Did you ever stop to think why so many American males have this Casanova complex?" Margaret Tenhausen asked, and then answered her own question. "Isn't it because we maintain an artificial separation between boys and girls practically from birth, and build into the life pattern of male and female an artificial mystery. So mysterious that for most boys the very process of seeing a naked woman intimately means, in practice that he must be engaged to her or declare his undying love, and even then he gets to see her only in bits and pieces as she may let him remove this or that garment in the front seat of an automobile. You will note that I said intimately. The only recourse in our culture would be photographs in girlie magazines or burlesque if that is still available. This, of course works both ways except that girls are taught to feign lack of interest. Finally our modern young man gets married and the glamour prototype, the girls in the middle of *Playboy* or such magazines, that he has been nurtured on, doesn't jibe with his nice little Nellie in curlers or squatting on the toilet. Because he never quite shakes off his years of conditioning that girls should be big breasted, hippy, leggy, sex pots with a come hither look, he can't help but feel that around the next corner the picture book girl will come to life. The same kind of conditioning on a romantic basis with the latest movie star or pop singer is the fare fed to our nice little Nellies, and they too finally continue to believe that Rock Hudson or some such is at the end of the rainbow. At the same time the society which offered this erotic conditioning now tells them that further intimate interest in the opposite sex outside the marriage bed is verboten. Next step the psychiatric couch!"

"Would any of the unmarried couples here volunteer information as to how you have solved your sex life?" Phil asked.

There was a moment of silence while everybody looked at each other sheepishly. Finally, Betty Vincent, who was doing graduate work in sociology, said, "I'll answer you, Phil. As you know, Jim Salter and I have been going together for three years. Jim and I are by all criteria, except legal or church sanctification, married. In the past year we've made love in cars, in hotels, in motels, in the woods, in his room when his roommate was out, and once standing up in a telephone booth. Neither of us like it, but Jim's father is very set in his belief that education and marriage don't mix. They are two separate worlds. If Jim gets married, okay, it's his bed to lie in, but his father sees no reason from that minute on to supply any funds for education."

"That about sums it up," Jim said smiling at Betty. "Except that my father would say that frustration is good for you. It tests your mettle."

"He has plenty of company," Phil said. "Pitrim Sorokin of Harvard claims that the sexual restraint embodied in our religious cultural traditions is responsible for the great advance of Western Civilization. This is reasoning after the fact, of course, supplemented with the belief that primitive societies have not kept pace with modern civilization because of their loose sexual morals."

"We have a more current example with the Russians," Bill Kingsley, who was interning at Mass. General Hospital, said. "In the first phases of the Russian Revolution one of the concepts was complete sexual freedom. They finally had to abandon the idea. The revolutionists took several wives, or never married at all. Children didn't know who their fathers were, and for a period, up until about 1936, sex-pre-occupation diverted the citizens so greatly that they failed miserably in their various state plannings. Today, in a complete reversal, the sexual morals of the Russians are more sedate practically by state decree, than the Victorian age. Visiting Russians are horrified by the overt sex that peers at them from every corner of the United States."

"If you do any thorough studying of the Victorian age," Margaret said, "you will find that the era has two faces: one the outside mask which was indeed very prim and proper, and under the mask a world seething with loose morality that even today, in our country, has not been duplicated. In any event, Phil and I do agree that a society is possible which would have a much freer and happier sexual code than ours. The approach has to be different, that's all."

Phil smiled. "There are many ancient civilizations which had cultures which we still admire. Their sexual codes and ethic were simply not tainted with the concept of sin. While your history books avoid the subject, the Spartans, who united the City States in Greece, and held together their society for at least as long as the United States, permitted a very free commerce between the sexes. Before marriage girls and boys were freely naked with each other in the processions and festivals. After marriage, if her husband consented, a man might have intercourse with another man's wife without any jealousy occurring. According to Plutarch, often the purpose was to have children by another man's wife in the hopes of improving the offspring. In such a society the idea of adultery did not exist, and there certainly was no need for prostitution ... and, in fact, it did not exist.

"You can contrast this with Athens where sex in every category was freely available for purchase, and indulged in freely by the males. Their wives, of course, had little or no sexual freedom, but when we look with admiration to the Greek achievements, which were considerable, we should remember that in their patriarchal society (which was the only kind known at the time) there was no male sexual inhibition. Of course Sparta was in many respects what we would term a police state. Defiance of the sexual codes by the Spartans as they were promulgated by Lycurgus, probably meant swift and severe punishment. Margaret and I feel, perhaps along with Plato who was certainly influenced by Sparta in writing "The Republic," that a police state is not a prerequisite for a society where sexual inhibitions and frustrations no longer exist. We believe that men and women can be trained from youth to live in an uninhibited sexual environment and because of their sexual freedom, *not in spite of it*, could make greater strides forward on an intellectual and emotional basis than any society that has ever existed on this earth.

"As you know we have been studying the sexual mores of mankind for some years." Phil waved at the booklined walls. "Outside of the Kinsey and Vatican libraries, we may possibly have the largest library of books anywhere written about man, woman and sex. Since the first Kinsey report it has been almost impossible to keep abreast of the outpouring of books on sex from the nation's publishers. Why so many books? And why do they sell? Because the average individual somewhere in his mind feels that there is a better way ... a better way, not only to approach the sex act itself and his or her entire concepts about the meaning of sex, but also the environment of sex. Modern man is bitterly confused, and his search for a solution on these, now utterly and completely frank, books; has by and large not provided him with any answers. Love and sex has been hashed and rehashed, until it would seem that there is nothing left to say. The sad fact is that in this avalanche of material there has been little or no original thinking which would lead us out of our sexual morass."

Phil grinned. "I don't know whether I remember the passage exactly but didn't Emerson say, 'Our age is retrospective. It builds sepulchres of the fathers. Why should we not also enjoy an original relation to the Universe? Why should we not have a poetry and philosophy of insight, and not of tradition, and a religion by revelation to us and not a history of theirs? The sun shines today also. Let us demand our own works and laws and worship.' "

"Phil is preparing you for the worse," Margaret interrupted smiling. "You see we have come to the conclusion that much of the sex tension and the sex problems in Western Society could be resolved by a program of education that actually educates the male and female into a deep understanding of the meaning of love ... an understanding so thoroughly inculcated, I might add, that each individual would approach another individual with an ability to stand aside from his own ego and simultaneously look at himself through the eyes and mind of the other person."

"I think that Ashley Montagu said something like that," Donna Friedman, who was doing graduate work in sociology, said. "Oh dear, I wish I could remember it."

Phillip quickly pulled a volume from the bookcase. "The book, Donna, is called *The Meaning of Love* ... it's a book that should have been read much more widely than it has been." Phillip flipped the pages. "Here is Montagu's summation: 'The most important thing to realize about the nature of human nature is that the most

143

significant ingredient in its structure is love. The church had recognized this, scientists are beginning to realize it but it will be the educators of the world to whom this task will fall not only of explaining the nature of love, but of teaching its meanings to the citizens of future generations. When that time arrives we will for the first time in the history of the Western World have truly educated human beings among us.' " Phillip paused. "The problem for the world is that up to now we have seen the need but the solutions are painfully slow in coming."

"Good heavens, Phil," Bill Kingsley said. "You are certainly giving us a build-up. In a few sentences what is the Harrad College Project? ... What and where is Harrad College? I've never heard of it."

"The build-up is somewhat essential," Phil said. "In a few sentences we believe that man desperately needs to develop a new sexual ethic and morality that coincides with life as it is today. To do this we are going to have to break radically with many of the mores of our culture. The final result could be a happy, responsible, sexually vital society gradually emerging and balancing the rapidly developing decadence of the past sixty years. A counter-revolution in a sense. The first step in our program would be a new kind of educative process for boys and girls commencing with their first year of college.

"But let me ramble for a few moments. The Harrad College Program will be an experiment in matching a male and female as potential marriage partners and inculcating them with a planned program of pre-marital sexual education and actual pre-marital living. This may shock you. If you aren't particularly shockable, and not many are left in the world today who are shocked by sex as such, then worse you may label it idealistic, and utopian. Any radical idea that departs from the standards of a particular time and place will create pressures from the outside that eventually will reshape the idea and make it conform to slow and more lasting changes. Yet, Margaret and I feel that the seeds of our idea have a great deal of validity, and gradually may scatter over the world, here and there taking root, and slowly effect a transformation in society. Moreover, we feel that this is a moral idea, and we set it hopefully against the moral bankruptcy of the world today.

"The idea that the root problem of Western Civilization can be solved by a new system of education based on sexual humanism offers democracies a challenging rebuttal to communism, and if adopted in the West would give a sense of purpose and direction that has been lacking in our conflict with communism. For example, what if the possibility of war were eliminated from the world tomorrow, and the Western democracies were suddenly free of the basic cause of their cohesiveness; a threatening Russia and China? I feel certain that without some substitute sense of social purpose that the Western democracies would gradually come apart at the seams. We in the United States would either have to turn to outer space to unify our society, or we would in the rapid growth of irresponsible leisure become a nation satiated with surface pleasure seeking. Man specifically, and in society, as a whole must be goal-seeking, and the nature of the goal must be worthwhile to him and constantly just beyond his reach. We are offering a plan and I use the word advisedly ... such a society must be planned ... an experiment in conditioning healthy teenagers in what Abraham Maslow of Brandeis calls 'self-actualization.' In our microcosmic society of Harrad College a program for each student will make him aware of his potentials, and will help him live his individual life for maximum realization of these potentials. In a sense, this program will encourage students to develop maximum curiosity, to explore and add to human knowledge, and make the learning process a lifetime challenge and limitless goal for each individual. In the process we plan to eliminate many of the shibboleths of sex and the tense relationship of males and females and substitute for them a new understanding of the importance of love."

"May I interrupt?" Jim Salter asked. "Isn't your program basically in line with the Christian point of view?"

"No," Phil said. "Not the Christian point of view. The Christ point of view, if you wish, which unfortunately is based primarily on emotion, and even more unfortunately is not a point of view which, despite all the lip service, has ever infiltrated into the average Christian's life. The Christian religion as practiced by Christians is a religion of expediency. We adjust the ultimate to fit every day of life. Ultimate verities, if there are any, in the Christian belief are made to comform to the requirements of the moment. Hence we pray to a Christian God to defeat our enemies, or expect God to forgive our sins and use absolution as a way out of our problems.

"A few years ago, the editors of *Life Magazine*, recognizing that the democracies, well-filled and satiated with goods, were not providing moral leadership in the world, called upon various nationally respected individuals to attempt to discover a National Purpose for the United

States. From this series came many platitudes, as well as recognition that man demanded more from life than the 'pursuit of happiness' ... especially a happiness based on the pursuit of material and sensual pleasures, but no thinker seemed able or willing to advance a centralizing concept for United States or Western Man that proposed an over-riding sense of mission strong enough or valid enough to answer the question that every man or woman eventually asks himself. 'Why am I here? Where am I going? What is the purpose of my life?'

"Now you may say that man can find the answers to these questions in the religion of his choice, but today, of necessity perhaps in our world, no religion can give man the answers which jibe with his secular life and the way he must live it. I feel that one of the reasons for the failure to achieve an answer is that being democratically oriented, and believing somehow or other that man in the mass in the long run will do right and find answers for individual man, our leaders are basically afraid to admit that this is not true. A particular social system, if it is to survive, must inherently offer the means to answer these questions. Democratic man may have to learn in the social as well as the economic realm that a dynamic society must have leaders who are beneficent dictators. Men who can envision the emotional as well as the economic goals for society. Because Margaret and I are as afraid of any kind of dictatorship as you are we are proposing the even more difficult proposition of a highly educated aristocracy functioning within the framework of democracy and guiding it by example and precept.

"I know I'm raving, Margaret," Phil said goodnaturedly when she tried to interrupt him. "But I sincerely am worried about the West's inability to provide strong emotional direction for the individual. The Russians have an answer and state it for individual Russians with a breathtaking simplicity. I'd like to read you an excerpt from the Third Program of the Communist Party, published in August of 1961. In the long haul if Russia manages to get rid of the idea that she is in conflict with the world on an ideological basis and confines her efforts to her homeland the repercussions of this kind of thinking being promulgated by an all powerful State and backed by a force which the church does not have in Western societies ... will inevitably, like it or not, affect the lives of your grandchildren setting as it does a moral framework and guide lines for the individual. Listen to this:

"*The Affirmation of Communist Morality*. In the

course of transition to Communism, the moral principles of society become increasingly important; the sphere of action of the moral factor expands and the importance of the administrative control of human relations diminishes accordingly. The Party will encourage all forms of conscious civil self discipline leading to the assertion and promotion of the basic rules of the communist way of life.

" 'The Communists reject the Class Morality of the exploiters; in contrast to the perverse, selfish views and morals of the old world, they promote communist morality which is the noblest and most just morality, for it expresses the interests and ideals of the whole of working mankind. Communism makes the elementary standards of morality and justice, which were shamelessly flouted under the power of exploiters, inviolable rules for relations both between individuals and between peoples. Communist morality encompasses the fundamental norms of human morality which the mass of the people evolved in the course of millenniums as they fought against vice and social oppression. The revolutionary morality of the working class is of particular importance to the moral advancement of society. As socialist and communist construction progresses, communist morality is enriched with new principles, a new content.

" 'The Party holds that *the moral code of the builder of communism* (italics theirs) should comprise the following principles:

" '(1) Devotion to the Communist cause; love of the socialist motherland, and of other socialist countries;

" '(2) Conscientious labour for the good of society—he who does not work, neither shall he eat;

" '(3) Concern on the part of everyone for the preservation and growth of public wealth;

" '(4) A high sense of public duty; intolerance of actions harmful to the public interest;

" '(5) Collectivism and comradely mutual assistance; one for all and all for one;

" '(6) Humane relations and mutual respect between individuals—man is to man a friend, comrade and brother;

" '(7) Honesty and truthfulness, moral purity, modesty and unpretentiousness in social and private life;

" '(8) Mutual respect in the family, and concern for the upbringing of children;

" '(9) An uncompromising attitude to injustice, parasitism, dishonesty and careerism;

" '(10) Friendship and tolerance among all the peoples of the U.S.S.R.; intolerance of national and racial hatred;

" '(11) An uncompromising attitude to the enemies of communism, peace and freedom of nations;

" '(12) Fraternal solidarity with the working people of all countries, and with all peoples.'

"As you think about these principles," Phil said, "envision the President of the United States or the Congress attempting to promulgate a moral order for the people of this country. Impossible! Any moral or ethical program proposed by a democratic government would meet with severe attack. In a democracy morals are, of course, left largely to the home and church.

"Unfortunately, the pronouncements of strong central government have historically carried the force of law, and as a result affect the citizens far beyond similar exhortations of the church or synagogue. It is almost as if the individual in the West expects that his rabbi or priest or minister will preach on a high moral plane but that this preaching is a kind of hot house plant that cannot stand the cold winds of everyday life.

"Whether it is ultimately successful or not Russian Communism is actively attempting to blend the moral, ethical and political order into a code of conduct and living that unites the inherent necessity of the individual to function in a goal-seeking environment. We, in the democracies, blithely accepting moral preaching as a Sabbath occupation to be tempered by the reality that man on a secular plane is lower than the animals, may well take heed. The individual communist with his religion, politics and morals emanating from one source is taught to conceive of himself as a superior citizen to the deviating democrat who pursues a winding course on both sides of the street."

"One point that I think you should make," Margaret said, "and it is something that is not generally realized, the Russians and the individual Russian has completely escaped the influence of Freud. Freud's writings are completely prohibited in Russia. Why? Because from the Russian point of view all of Freud's teachings and 'discoveries' carry a stigma that man is the prey of his emotions, that conscious man reacts unconsciously as the result of forces, the id, ego, superego and libido, which are inescapable and beyond his control. From the Russian viewpoint we have reaped the reward. Our Christian and Jewish inheritance coupled with the dominance of Freudian thinking in our society negates the individual as a master of his destiny and creates a sense of hopelessness. For the past twenty years our writers have portrayed man swimming in the sewerage of a fate from which he can't escape. Contrast this with the Russians who have glorified Pavlov as the psychologist of Russia and the basic Pavlovian belief that man can be conditioned, that man can create an environment which will permit him to achieve the stars both literally and figuratively. The problem facing Western democracies is: Can we give each individual citizen confidence, hope and goals that are not based in materialism, and do this without the outer direction of a powerful state? Phil and I believe that it can be done, but it means that democratic man will have to lift himself by his boot straps, and it will be the educators of this country who must define the goal.

"Where is our world now?" Margaret asked. She took a sheaf of clippings from a box beside her chair. "Let me read some of these to you rapidly without rhyme or reason, because that is the way the average citizen of a democracy encounters them in a week. They are not a-typical, and you can very easily gather your own collection of a similar material. The question is: Is there a common denominator that might point up an alchemist's solution to the sad hopeless environment that makes things like these a way of life for millions of people in the world?"

Margaret read rapidly, choosing at random newspaper, magazine and direct mail clippings that she had evidently been accumulating:

" 'Five rapists sentenced to life imprisonment today in the gang assault of a pretty blonde captive.

" 'The five who got life terms all had pleaded guilty to rape charges. The nineteen year old girl is the daughter of a chemical firm executive. Her identity was not disclosed by the court to protect her reputation.

" 'The mass rape occurred in a lovers' lane in nearby Leominster while her boyfriend, a one-time Dartmouth student, was held captive. . . .'

" 'Your new way of life begins at Key Colony Beach! All of this can be yours for only $8500. Yes, for this low price plus a nominal fee of only $35 per month for maintenance and upkeep, you can have your own completely furnished apartment.

" 'On the left you see a typical Golf Club apartment, and on the right a panoramic view of your neighborhood at the Golf Club apartments. A Polynesian atmosphere is captured at the entrance with a large waterfall and a hand-carved Tiki from the South Seas. To the left of the Club House is a thirty-foot replica of an island volcano which is the center of many happy outdoor cook-outs. Everything here is designed for your pleasure. Everything is taken care of for you. When you live in the Golf Club apartments you leave your worries behind. Your taxes are paid, your insurance is kept up to date, your lawn is cut and your hedges are trimmed, all repairs are taken care of for you. All maintenance is taken care of. ... There is nothing left for you but to enjoy yourself!'

" 'Bill To Set Up Divorce Service Given Support. A bill to establish a divorce conciliation service on a trial basis in two counties today won considerable support at a public hearing ... The bill would require that when an application is made for divorce the parties be required to appear before a court-appointed family counselor who would attempt to resolve their differences. Judge Carl E. Wahlstrom made an urgent plea for the passage of the bill and told of his experience with divorce while sitting for twenty-one years on the bench. "I have heard 12,000 divorce cases, a record that I am not particularly proud of. The statistics show that about two children are involved in each divorce, which means that I alone have touched the lives of 50,000 people in broken homes." Judge Wahlstrom said 700–800 divorces are granted each year in Worcester County. He said a survey he made showed that 251 divorces were now on the public welfare and 25% of them had an illegitimate child since their divorce.'

" 'From a book service. Olympia Selections, descriptions of current book offerings. *The Sword and the Promise*. Sadistic, Roman soldiers torture and kill innocent men and women. Those not killed are brought to the slave market where they are sold to the highest bidder and branded like cattle. *Naked Before My Captors*. This story thunders to an exciting climax when Colonel Forant uncovers the shocking extent of his wife's infidelities. Brent Dahlgren is brutally beaten by Otto's hired bully, and Lilly is brutally manhandled. *Jack the Ripper* (an actual quotation from this book). "She tried to shake her head. The man's free hand closed over the neck of her dress and with a fierce jerk the material was torn away. She struggled feebly but his eager hand clutched at the cotton petticoat. She felt the tug and the tearing of the washworn fabric. The cool fog touched her bare shoulder. Her hand flew up to cover her breast, but her assailant knocked her hand away and his fingers began to fondle the soft sensitive mounds of her flesh. A thin line of spittle appeared at the corner of his mouth. He stared down at the melon curve of her breast lying in the gloved palm, and in his pre-occupation eased the pressure on her throat." '

" 'This Rotted World. *Time Magazine:* "Many serious liberal minded intellectuals worry profoundly about the unattractive impression the U.S. often makes abroad, blaming everyone from unimaginative ambassadors to loud tourists with star-spangled sports shirts. But few would admit that some of their own heroes—for example Tennessee Williams—can be the worst ambassador of all ... The most telling indictment (of Tennessee Williams' plays *Sweet Bird of Youth* and *Suddenly Last Summer*) was written by critic Henrique Oscar (critic for *Diario de Noticias*, a Rio de Janeiro newspaper). Oscar brushed aside the Method and the visiting (U.S. Government sponsored) production to go after Tennessee Williams himself and the psycheburger school of playwriting. 'People bearing vices can be presented provided they suffer from them,' wrote Oscar. 'Their suffering may redeem them and arouse our understanding if not sympathy. The morbid world of Tennessee Williams has nothing of this. With him aberration is presented complacently with all the author's tenderness, as if it were the best thing in the world. It is sad to think that Williams represents a country which is Western and "Christian" whose style of life they want to convince us should be defended against the Communist threat. Positively this rotted world does not seem worthy of defending, and on the contrary needs to be reformed or extinguished so that something may survive to preserve man's intrinsic dignity.' "

" '*What's Nude?* A photograph cartoon book published by Ivan Obolensky using photographs of female nudes plus a cartoon of what purports to be a Mr. Playboy in his middle sixties imagining the female buttocks as a balloon jib on a sailboat, the female breasts a ski-jump, nude female dolls that wind up available 2 for 49¢, nude female rocking chairs, nude female drapes, nude female bowling pins, etc., etc. From the introduction by Nathaniel Benchley: "But if she had been given some research (Grandma) she would have been surprised to discover that what men think about most is women—in the abstract or in the particular, dressed or undressed, friendly or unfriendly, tame or untamed. Of course not all men think about women in the same way. There are the Droolers and the Epicures, the Collectors and the Haters, the Cowed and the Condescending, but no matter what attitude a man takes on the subject he cannot escape their all pervading presence." '

"Whew," Margaret said puffing, "that's enough! It isn't that I like the sound of my own voice. I could read you hundreds more. When you pick up your newspaper tomorrow, or look at your television dramas, or read your magazines, you'll find man, God's ultimate creation, wallowing and sinking in sewerage of a world he never made. Why is it that night and day throughout the year, in most democratic countries, that the unhappy deviating sexual problems of men and women are the spice that makes the daily ennui and boredom with life palatable unto the grave? The story in the evening paper of the five rapists can be multiplied to infinity. Rape, murder, adultery, homosexuality, every brutal, or what is considered abnormal relationship of man to man and woman to man is reported with utmost fidelity in the nation's press, picture magazines, and even women's magazines who wring their hands over the sexual morass, but at the same time chew each manifestation over lasciviously as potent circulation builders.

"Nowhere in this mass of reportage is there any attempt to get behind the individual facts and find why the offenders against society or against the sexual mores are in this particular predicament. Moralizing in depth is left for the psychiatrist and the psychologist or the general educator who the mass of men never read. The preacher vacillates between Original Sin or the hope of a sexless heaven, and hundreds of novelists since Joyce and Hemingway and Faulkner feel that their duty is to mirror a world where for the most part men and women are consigned to a moral pig-sty where they blindly copulate."

Margaret paused and Jim Salter said, "Margaret ... Phil, Good God . . . I think all of us here accept your comments on the social situation. Let's get back to this panacea solution of yours. It sounds like a pipe dream ... permitting kids to copulate freely would solve all the world's problems? Oh, brother!"

Phil grinned. "Margaret and I are old-time tub thumpers ... just give me a few more minutes to put our idea in perspective and then we'll give you the floor." Phil flipped the pages of the typewritten manuscript he kept referring to. "I'm not planning to read this entire manuscript to you, but this section is of some importance in setting the scene for what we are doing.

"We believe," Phil read, "that all human beings tend

toward a monogamous relationship, and the only thing fundamentally wrong with monogamy is that it is too constricting, and lacks the necessary element of adventure which is a natural human characteristic. As has been pointed out by many scholars we are in a period of schizophrenia in our moral and sexual relationships. Man believes that what his laws, his state, his church preach and advocate for sexual behavior, both in and out of marriage, are eternal verities, and yet man, himself is unable to live a life based on these standards. What are some of these moral standards? Society projects the idea that a girl or boy, despite his or her awakening sexuality at the age of sixteen or seventeen, should somehow or other live a life of inhibited sexual desires until marriage, and when married should live in perfect harmony, sexual and otherwise, with one individual for the rest of his life. Deviations from this pattern are both sinful and illegal.

"What is the result? A society so inhibited that the only thing left open to them is the sex-tease; a continuous tickling of the sex sensibilities of the average maturing person with no gratification for years, and when gratification is achieved, often a failure of reality to measure up to the whetted appetite.

"We have on the one hand teen-age marriages at an alarming rate counterbalanced with a divorce pattern that is frightening in its meaning to society as a whole.

"We have a society where the disseminators of entertainment, the novelists, the movie and television producers, the dramatists pander to our repressed sexuality, while we read and view and revel in this world of unleashed sexuality until our continuous daydreaming and trifling with unreality creates a situation that populates our mental hospitals to the bursting point.

"Like starving men we eat the sawdust, vomit and feebly attempt to return to the abnormal asceticism that our culture says is the true, the moral, the upstanding way of life.

"There will be no cure until man is actually educated that his God-driven desire for happy, healthful sexual coupling is natural and good. The problem and the solution revolves around the question: Can society be reoriented into responsible sexual and marriage patterns permitting free sexual expression, which could result in happy and meaningful marriage and family relationships with built in responsibility to society?

"We believe that the average male and female relationship goes through three interacting phases and that these phases can be planned to offer sexual varietism. This could be accomplished by a definitive program of educating the male and female for a full life with each other, and a more complete and more deeply shared life for each individual. To develop such a program we must set higher emotional standards for man as a whole. It is a commonplace that our scientific and intellectual growth has far outpaced our emotional grasp of life. This has occurred not because of lack of human ability but lack of emphasis on mature emotional development. We believe for example that human beings can be conditioned and taught human love does not have to be a one-to-one relationship from teen-age to the grave. A man or woman can actually without fear, or jealousy, love two or more people simultaneously without a sense of exclusiveness or ownership that might destroy the relationship. Jealousy is an outworn and primitive concept which has no validity among educated men. Pre-marital sexual intercourse, properly conceived within a controlled situation is a healthy normal relationship. Post-marital sexual relationships now labelled as sinful and unforgiveable, can actually exist concomitantly with a monogamous marriage. Individuals can be educated for happy adjustment in marriages that give them expanded interpersonal sexual relationships.

"The first phase of the male and female relationship, instead of being a time of frustration and unfulfilled yearnings for the opposite sex, will be a period of orientation and the development of a 'life-plan' for the individual. In keeping with the discoveries of modern psychology, the teenager will learn the purposive aspects of his individual 'self,' and will actually be taught how to relate the many individual aspects of his psychological 'selfs' into a harmonious whole.

"As a pilot program the Harrad College Pre-Marital Living Program has enrolled a carefully chosen group of late teen-age boys and girls in a four year college program. During these four years instead of pursuing our current educational policy of artificially separating male and female students, or worse, separating them completely on specific college campuses, Harrad College will offer a plan where a carefully selected boy will live in the same college dormitory room with a carefully selected girl enjoying as complete or limited sexual relationships as they may desire."

"Hold on a minute, Phil!" Jim Salter said. "You've changed tenses. Up to this time you have been offering this as a proposal. Now you are saying 'has enrolled.' You mean you have sold this wacky idea to someone?"

Margaret smiled. "Remember, all of you gathered here are our trusted inner circle. We do not want publicity at this stage. A year ago, as Bob Rimmer knows, the Carnsworth Foundation gave us a grant of ten million dollars to develop our program. The campus of Harrad College is very near completion on fifty acres of the old Carnsworth Estate just outside Cambridge. The freshman class of fifty male and fifty female students is enrolled and will occupy the dormitories in September."

There was an audible gasp from everyone in the room. Questions expressing disbelief flew fast and thick.

"Phil ... Margaret!" Donna Friedman said. "You can't be serious! What you have been saying is one thing as theory, and something else again as a practical program. It's illegal. The law won't permit it!"

"Where did you ever find parents to agree?" Betty Vincent gasped. "You would never have sold the idea to my mother that her virgin daughter would move in and live with a man. Unmarried? Wow! Even my father agrees that men are no good and just have one thing on their minds. A girl has to sell what she's got quick before the bloom fades."

"You actually mean that a boy and a girl will sleep in the same room together?" Bill Kingsley chuckled. "Phil, you must have been smoking hashish. Do you really think they would ever study?"

"The girl would be pregnant before mid-years!" Jim Salter said.

Phil chuckled. "Let me answer Betty's question first. Admittedly this took some planning. Over the past years since we have been tentatively proposing such an idea, we have naturally picked up, not only in the United States but in many parts of the world, a group of interested and enthusiastic followers. When John Carnsworth decided to implement the program financially, our first step was to contact very carefully prospective parents who might be interested. It took up the better part of a year, but we exceeded our expectations. We lined up more than three hundred prospective candidates about equally divided as to sex. These prospectives were examined as thoroughly as it is possible for psychologists to examine and probe into the inner life of an individual. In the process we developed a complete documentation of the emotional and intellectual lives of our candidates as well as a tremendous amount of information on their family background. Working with one of the large data processing organizations we programmed this entire material and then, working on the theory that 'opposites may attract but similars marry,' we correlated the most likely girl for the most likely boy."

"Oh, Phil, that's terrible!" Donna Friedman said. "You are saying in effect that working with your computing machines you can pick out marriage partners. What happens to romance?"

"We are not especially picking them for marriage partners. They are not coming to Harrad College specifically to get married. We do believe, however, that ultimately a large percentage of our choices will marry. Furthermore, Betty, we believe that romance and love develops rapidly between similars. Perhaps you have found your one and only in Jim Salter, and he in you. We believe, however, that if that be true, it is a lucky accident. We do not believe that you and Jim, for example, are the only possible mates for each other. We feel that exposed to our testing and given a wide enough sample, particularly when you were in your late teens and hence in your more formative years, that we could have located and mated you with a fairly large number of possible members of the opposite sex with whom you would have been supremely happy."

"Perhaps we can make this a little more specific," Margaret said. "Let me give you a typical example of a boy and girl who will live together at Harrad. Stanley is the boy. He was born in Detroit. His family are first generation Poles in this country. He has four sisters. The family is very poor. His father works on the assembly line at one of the automobile companies. Stanley is a brilliant student. He is coming to Harrad on a Carnsworth complete scholarship grant. His basic interests are history and government. While his family has little or no education, he was fortunate in school to have a Polish teacher who took a great deal of interest in him and stimulated him. Stanley has read widely. He taught himself to play the piano and could become an expert musician. Stanley is quite introspective, however. His piano playing seems to be a need to express his almost inarticulate longings to understand love or beauty in the world. Stanley is quite handsome. While he is only eighteen he fell in love with a girl from a family with a much higher income level. The girl and Stanley had sexual relations at least once, and the girl wanted to marry him. Stanley was agreeable, but the girl's parents effectively put their foot down. The girl was enrolled in a college near Los Angeles.

"The girl Stanley will live with at Harrad is Sheila. Sheila is eighteen and three months. Sheila someday will be a very lovely woman. At the moment she is completely unaware of her essential beauty. She wears sloppy clothes. She dresses haphazardly, usually in floppy sweaters and tweedy skirts. I would guess that on the surface she is probably just the opposite of the girl Stanley was in love with. Sheila graduated Summa Cum Laude from a co-ed academy in Connecticut. In addition she won all the prizes in English. Sheila hopes to major in sociology. Sheila's father is a millionaire. He is married to his third wife. Sheila's mother lives happily in Connecticut, with her second husband who is a poorly paid accountant. Sheila's love is her father, but he is too busy and is too involved in his own affairs to give her much love in return. Her mother has had several children by her second husband. While Sheila has a room in her mother's home, Sheila doesn't feel comfortable there. The fact is that Sheila really has no home. Her life thus far has probably made her quite introspective. She has thus retreated into the world of knowledge . . . almost as a form of escape. Sheila is a virgin. Probably not by choice. Her high marks and general sloppiness probably isolated her from any predatory young men. Incidentally, Sheila also is a competent pianist. She took lessons for ten years. Today, she seldom plays the piano."

"Ye Gods," Bill Kingsley said. "You mean these two will room together? Outside of playing the piano they seem to be completely unlike."

"We know a lot more about them, Bill," Phil said. "You would have to study their various tests thoroughly. The surface aspects may be somewhat different . . . underneath Sheila and Stanley are twin personalities."

"What's going to stop them from jumping into bed with each other?" Jim Salter asked. "Maybe you'd like to explain more fully the sexual aspects of the daydream?"

"Eventually, we expect and hope that they may," Margaret said laughing. "Not at first. Possibly not at all, although that's unlikely. You see, Jim, Sheila and Stanley, as well as all the students selected for Harrad College, understand that they are involved in a mature and responsible relationship. An adventure in understanding another individual and adjusting to him or her. Our introductory courses at Harrad will give each student a thorough knowledge of contraception. When and if a couple decide to have sexual relations they will understand that a pregnancy would force an immediate marriage, and probably an end to their college career. Every aspect of our conditioning program for Harrad students will re-emphasize constantly that the sexual relationship is a responsible act entered into with love in its true sense. We believe that the act of sexual intercourse should be regarded not as an ultimate way for an individual to break the bonds that bind him to his or her 'self,' but as *one* way. The other way is complete communication between the many selves of one person with the many selves of another. This is a lifetime pursuit. Some of our science fiction writers speak of an age when mental telepathy will be an actuality. Love as we envision it developing properly would be a continual search into separateness of people. Every man *is* an island and the greatest drive in any individual psyche is to break out of that island. At Harrad we will try to show them how. When we finish the dream of science fiction will be very much a reality. These individuals who are roommates and even those who are not roommates but have been through the Harrad experience may actually learn to communicate telepathically."

"You may not realize it," Phil continued. "Working together as closely as we have in our fifteen years of marriage, Margaret and I have actually accomplished this on a daily basis. In areas completely disassociated from the work we are doing we often know exactly what the other is thinking. But leaving that aside, let's examine what we feel will actually occur between our typical students, Sheila and Stanley. In the first few weeks of their new relationship they will be extremely shy with each other. However, we predict that within a month this shyness will break down rapidly. In addition to the Physical Education program which will, following Greek custom, be in the nude, each floor of the Harrad dormitories will have communal bathing facilities. Thus students living on a particular floor will freely see each other naked. Each room of the Harrad dormitory will have a study room, a bedroom with twin beds and a toilet with a bidet. We feel that in the area of elimination and douching, the individual in our society is conditioned from birth to maintain a sense of privacy, and nothing is to be gained from breaking this down unless it occurs spontaneously. After several weeks, Sheila and Stanley will probably dress and undress in front of each other with great unconcern. Because they are in an unusual environment the subject of sex will be a continual topic of discussion, not only as they seek out the fundamentals of their own existence but in the groups and in the friendships they will make with other students. However, don't over emphasize the sexual aspects. We are conditioned in our society that when we put a male and female together that sex is the by-product. It is inconceivable to us that sex doesn't have to be the single focal point of their relationship. Remember that Sheila and Stanley will be immediately plunged into high pressure accelerated courses of study. To continue at Harrad they will be well aware that they must maintain a very high standard of marks in the courses of study, of their own choosing, that they will pursue. These are not empty headed teen-agers confined in a room and mooning at each other."

At this point on the tape Phil moved the discussion away from the sexual elements of life at Harrad, and involved all of us in a detailed analysis of his pivotal course in Human Values required of all Harrad students.

It was nearly two in the morning when we left the Tenhausens. Despite the hour, Jim Salter seemed reluctant to end the discussion. "Honestly, Phil and Margaret, the whole idea seems incredible to me ... it makes all the Utopias I have ever read and all the ideas on communal living, including Oneida and Brook Farm, seem like kindergarten exercises by comparison. In those experiments there was some attempt at a cohesive factor, religion or something else to hold the participants in line. Your daydream is too fluid ... too democratic. It will run amok. Let me give you an example of what I mean. Say it is now November. Harrad College has been functioning ... you hope ... for two months. In addition to Sheila and Stanley you have forty-nine other couple groupings. Here's a few of the situations, offhand, that could materialize ... Given time I could probably give you twice as many:

"(1) Neither Sheila nor Stanley care enough for each other to sleep together, yet they are caught in the web of a little world where free love is the password.

"(2) Sheila falls in love with Stanley but not vice versa.

"(3) Stanley falls in love with Sheila but not vice versa.

"(4) One or the other gets mixed up with some other couple grouping who are not enjoying the same happy 'love' circumstance and try to disrupt Sheila's and Stanley's 'love.'

"(5) They have coitus and it's so easy and unrestrained without guilt that they get bored with it. It lacks meaning.

"(6) It turns out that Stanley is a man's man, he likes to have sex ... on the run so to speak ... but not as a way of life. This commitment of having a female roommate is too much akin to actual marriage.

"(7) Sex, and the opposite sex, is so freely available that the whole thing becomes debased currency.

"(8) After a little bit of free sex Sheila decides she wants to hold Stanley by fair means or foul and lets herself become pregnant.

"I could go on," Jim said, coming up for air, "but that is plenty, you can multiply it by forty-nine, and quadruple it, if you ever manage to get a complete freshman, sophomore, junior and senior class functioning at Harrad College."

Phil smiled. We were all standing near his front door. "Jim," he said. "Everything you say is true . . . not only for Harrad College but life in general. We have come thousands of years from the primitive cavemen rubbing their sticks together to make fire. We can now create a holocaust of fire that threatens to destroy the world. Yet with all his marvelous control of nature and the elements, man's control of his emotions and his personal knowledge of himself and other men have been painfully slow. When you stop to think about it, perhaps in a wider perspective this was necessary if society was ever to have progressed this far. Philosophy begins with full bellies. It is only a few generations, and in some cases a few decades, that most men have arrived at a juncture where they no longer have to growl at their neighbor as they go in search of sustenance. But amazingly, through all the recorded history of strife, hatred, wars, envy, jealousy, certain thinkers such as Confucius, Buddha, Ramakrishna, Socrates, Jesus, and thousands of unsung men have added their words to a growing chorus that in the next hundred years may finally prove that individual men can master their emotions.

"We believe that we do have a common denominator in the Harrad Program. We are stacking the cards in our favor by selecting only emotionally and intellectually superior people. Using this fertile ground we believe that will be successful. Instead of waiting for the few great and wise men that inevitably emerge in each generation, Margaret and I believe that if we are successful we will inculcate these ideas as a way of life for hundreds of men and women. From hundreds will come thousands and within a hundred years the mathematical odds will be in our favor. In the twenty-first or twenty-second century, men everywhere will live who have learned the meaning of man and love. If we fail, you can't say that it hasn't been worth trying!"